THE ART OF GIG

THE ART OF GIG

VOLUME 1 | FOUNDATIONS

VENKATESH RAO

RIBBONFARM.COM

ISBN 978-1-959228-00-4 (paperback)

ISBN 978-1-959228-02-8 (ebook)

Cover illustration and design by Grace Witherell. Produced by Jenna Dixon.

ribbonfarm.com

CONTENTS

PREFACE

This book is the first of two volumes of collected essays from *The Art of Gig* weekly email newsletter, which I wrote between 2019 and 2021. The title, as well as the general perspective, were inspired by Sun Tzu's classic, *The Art of War*. I aspired to write about the gig economy in a way that would showcase its sublime, poetic side, while also providing an unflinching look at its darker side. I don't know to what degree I succeeded, but it did me good to try.

The newsletter was mostly about internet-enabled independent or "indie" consulting, though I occasionally ventured further afield to other parts of the gig economy. When I retired the newsletter in 2021, I had been in the gig economy for a decade, having left my last paycheck job at Xerox in early 2011. These two volumes are the result of the first decade of my own experiences as an independent consultant, with perhaps a few dozen clients.

I like to think *The Art of Gig* newsletter helped seed what is now a thriving online conversation around indie consulting. Surprisingly, even though this kind of gig work has been a thing since at least 1999, it only turned into a genuine scene around 2016 or so. I suspect the growing maturity and sophistication of the "creator stack" is at least partly responsible.

While I have done my best to extract and share the most general lessons I can from my experiences, these essays necessarily reflect the idiosyncrasies of my own path. You should seek out other sources for triangulation, and think through and test out my ideas in the context of your own situation. Uncritical adoption of career advice is significantly more hazardous in the gig economy than it is in the paycheck economy.

In particular, much of my work has been with medium to large technology companies in North America, though I have on occasion worked with clients in Europe and Latin America, and also with a few early-stage startups. Almost all my work has been one-on-one work with senior executives, in particular in a mode I call *executive sparring* (covered in the final section in this volume). To the extent your circumstances are different from mine, be careful what conclusions you draw from what I have to say.

This volume includes the essays from the newsletter that cover foundational topics, divided into six themed sections. It should be of value if you're contemplating, or just getting started with, an independent consulting career. It should also be helpful if you've been independent for a while, but have struggled to find your footing, and want to reflect on foundational issues.

The second volume contains more advanced material, and should be of value to those who have developed a good feel for the foundations and are looking to explore beyond them.

All the essays have been carefully edited and updated for these volumes, and in a few cases, significantly rewritten. Many of the original illustrations accompanying the essays have been redrawn.

A few pandemic-themed essays, originally published in the newsletter in early 2020, during the first couple of months of the pandemic, have been dropped.

The newsletter, during its run, also featured a series of speculative fiction pieces, set in an imaginary consulting milieu called the

Yakverse. The Yakverse stories are *not* included in this two-volume set. I have different, more experimental plans for that material.

I owe a big debt of gratitude to the nearly 4,000 readers of the *Art of Gig* newsletter, and especially the several hundred subscribers who made it financially sustainable. Without their enthusiastic support and engagement through the life of the newsletter, and repeated demands for book compilations after it wound down, these two volumes would not have seen the light of day.

I am particularly thankful to the dozen or so readers with whom I kept up an active exchange of ideas through the life of the newsletter. Tom Critchlow and Paul Millerd, in particular, kept me on my toes.

Thanks to Jenna Dixon for her support in editing and producing these volumes and to Grace Witherell for supplying fine cover art. Thanks also to John Fuller and Miodrag Vujkovic for last-minute help with the copyediting.

And finally, thanks to my wife Meeyong for her steadfast and endlessly resourceful support through my tumultuous first decade as an indie consultant.

SECTION ONE

THE DEEP END

A story should have a beginning, a middle and an end, but not necessarily in that order.

JEAN-LUC GODARD

1

42 GREAT IMPERATIVES
WELL, HERE WE GO

I'M GOING to drop this conversation right into the deep end, with a list of 42 Great Imperatives of gigwork in general, and indie consulting in particular.

Niels Bohr defined a Great Truth as one whose negation is also a Great Truth. I've framed these as imperatives for your comfort and convenience, but the same principle applies. The opposite of every Great Imperative is also a Great Imperative.

If you like, give yourself 1 point for each of these that you either strongly agree with *or* disagree with based on your own experience and 0 points if it seems like an arbitrary or theoretical concern that you have no strong experience-based feelings about. Deduct 1 point if you can't even figure out what the hell I'm talking about with a particular point. Your total score is a measure of your Capability Maturity Level as a consultant. If you score less than 10, don't quit your day job. If you score less than 5, see a doctor to check if you are alive and over eighteen.

1. Do not accept work when broke that you would reject when flush.
2. Say yes or no to gigs against your instincts 10% of the time.
3. Never assign homework the client didn't ask for.
4. Never accept homework you didn't ask for.
5. Solve for industry-level questions, not organization- or world-level answers.
6. Choose hunting-party clients over individuals or impersonal organizations.
7. Never accept a deliverable request from an intermediary who can't act on it.
8. Create choices, not recommendations.
9. Keep your bespoke models as simple as possible.
10. Only use off-the-shelf models that you enjoy nerding out over.
11. Avoid making up vanity models.
12. Do not participate in execution except in ceremonial forms (like talks).
13. Do not participate in risk where you can manipulate the reward.
14. Avoid anchor clients.
15. Avoid polished deliverables.
16. Document through communication (such as email), not documents.
17. The work ends when the story ends, not when the last check clears.
18. Keep your private identity amusing to yourself.
19. Keep your public identity a 10-foot-pole away from your gigwork.
20. Keep your client-facing identity normie.
21. Do not claim unambiguous value addition amidst ambiguous outcomes.

22. Retrospectives of whole outcomes over personal value-addition estimates.
23. No more than 7±2 active cases at a time (and that's pushing it).
24. Train your memory to remember an hour of conversation without notes.
25. Don't trust your situation awareness in a gig after six months of inactivity.
26. Learn what's unique about the sector and its history.
27. Learn the sector's paper-napkin math and unique measures of itself.
28. Demystify the industry's science and technology stack for yourself.
29. Discourage use of purely internal jargon in how clients talk to you.
30. Keep the game in your head, not your head in the game.
31. Design your personal incentives to remove moral hazard.
32. Avoid sending unsolicited pitches.
33. Cost-plus accounting over value-based accounting.
34. If a client asks for an ROI estimate, walk away.
35. Do not accept money the client cannot afford to spend.
36. In billing, bundle and unbundle line items for at-a-glance auditability.
37. Avoid retainers and advances unless the client needs to use them.
38. Hourly rate over project or piece rate, project or piece rate over outcome-based.
39. Learn more from every client than they learn from you.
40. Learn to play obfuscated chess postman[1] across gigs, live.
41. Generalize what you learn for public consumption, but not too soon.
42. Never let the truth get in the way of a good story.

Why is this the deep end? Because you won't encounter the substance and reasoning behind these Great Imperatives until you're a few years and a half-dozen clients into indie consulting. Some of these will seem theoretical and/or unnecessarily down in the weeds to you. Others will seem arbitrary or overly philosophical.

I've violated every single one of these in the last decade, some of them multiple times. But I've followed each rule more often than I've violated it, so they are my defaults. What's more, they're neither idiosyncratic personal defaults, nor common-sense defaults that work well for everybody.

They are *good* defaults that undergird a particular philosophy and approach to indie consulting. They are the bedrock of the school of consulting I'm founding that will last ten thousand years and evolve into a Holy Order of Space Consultants and whose Original Immutable Esoteric Truths I will be sharing with those who prove themselves worthy.

Though of course the actual list of Great Imperatives is subject to Great Edits.

If I had brainstormed this list five years ago, it would have been different. If I brainstorm it again in five years, it will be different. But the Original Immutable Esoteric soul of the list would remain the same, through such regenerations of the verbal body. And there will always be exactly 42 Great Imperatives. No more, no less. Why? See Great Imperative 42.

Welcome to the Art of Gig.

---

1. Basically, *obfuscated chess postman* is applying learnings from one gig to another in real-time by creating suitable abstractions to port your new learnings without compromising confidentiality. The entire consulting industry is built around this.

2

ELEMENTS OF CONSULTING STYLE

CUSTOMERS BUY ONLY TWO THINGS: HAPPINESS AND SOLUTIONS TO PROBLEMS

WHILE THE SALES cliché is true—people really do only buy happiness or solutions to problems—as an indie consultant, you're very unlikely to be selling happiness (outside of certain types of speaking gigs where you might be the featured entertainment). Whatever the *content* of your services, whether it is corporate strategy, web design, M&A technical due diligence, survey design, market research, or copywriting, you are almost certainly selling *solutions to problems*. And the problems external consultants solve always fall into two basic buckets: *insufficient systematic confidence* and *insufficient systematic doubt*. If a problem does not fall into one of these two buckets, typically it will be solved by an employee, contractor, or a b2b product/service. Any consultants present will be seen as parasites to be exterminated rather than utilized more. A part of the problem rather than the solution.

Each of these two classes of problems can exist at two loci relative to the client: in their *outer world* or their *inner world*. That gives us four basic types of clients (both individuals and organizations) and four kinds of consultants they typically hire, as shown in the 2x2 on the next page. Take a look, tag yourself, and let's unpack this.

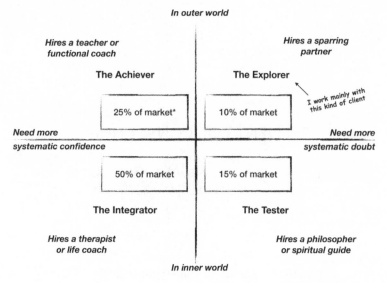

| The Four Types of Clients

THE FOUR TYPES OF CLIENTS—INDIVIDUAL

As a consultant, your identity and style are derived from your client's identity and style: your persona is a *shadow* persona. So the four types of clients induce four different basic shadow identities and styles of consulting. Of course, no client is a pure or constant example of a single type, so no consultant is a pure or constant example of a single type of shadow.

The Explorer is a client who wants to build capacity for systematic doubt at an outer-world locus. They do this by constantly considering possibilities, alternative perspectives, and refactorings of worldviews. They tend to hire a sparring partner type of consultant who can constantly stress test their thinking and actions, and undermine their assumptions from unexpected new directions.

The Achiever is a client who wants to build systematic confidence at an outer-world locus. They typically hire consultants who take on roles as teachers or coaches, helping them develop specific functional capabilities and skills, such as public speaking, survey methodology, being more productive, architecting databases, running Kickstarter campaigns, applying for government grants, or sourcing things from China.

The Integrator is a client who wants to build systematic confidence at an inner-world locus. Whether or not they choose to explicitly acknowledge it, they look for an element of therapy or life coaching in their relationships with consultants they hire. Whatever the nominal subject—better relationships at work, faster time to market, improved sales conversions—the actual focus for the Integrator client is always building a better integrated psyche.

The Tester is a client who wants to build systematic doubt at an inner-world locus. They do this by constantly testing their thinking, questioning their assumptions about themselves, and introspecting on their actions. Don't mistake all the testing for an empiricist or exploratory orientation though. The Tester is primarily looking for meaning in a philosophical sense. The ambiguities and uncertainties they are probing are primarily within them. Their experiential experiments are about discovering themselves.

I estimate—and this is a pure guess based on anecdotal evidence and notes swapped with fellow consultants—that about half the demand for consulting services is from Integrators. The smallest market is Explorers. Achiever and Tester markets are in between. This is my read on *individual* demand, whether personal or situated within an organization.

THE FOUR TYPES OF CLIENTS—ORGANIZATIONS

The four types can also be used to anthropomorphically characterize *organizational* personalities in relation to the types of independent consultants they like to hire (large consulting firms serve a different kind of need, with a broader footprint, that doesn't map well here).

This organizational personality is often, but not always, an extension of the personality of founders or powerful senior leaders (who may be long dead or retired).

The Explorer Organization tends to be future-oriented and is likely to have people or departments devoted to activities such as scenario planning, futures, and market modeling (often called strategy operations). Explorer organizations hungrily consume forecasts and trend information, as well as historical analyses and industry reports. They believe they are *curious* organizations.

The Achiever Organization tends to be capabilities-focused and is likely to have a well-developed and staffed training organization running various sorts of structured training and coaching programs for all employees right up to executive level. Achiever organizations love building out corporate habits-and-processes infrastructure ranging from Lean Six Sigma for everybody to media/PR training for senior executives. They believe they are *winning* organizations.

The Integrator Organization tends to be employee mental health and culture focused. They love things like employee-engagement programs, well-being initiatives, and diversity and inclusion programs. You will find a strong culture of listening habits inside such organizations: town-halls, manager-employee 1:1s, and effective communication training. They believe they are *compassionate* organizations.

The Tester Organization is a relatively new type, since it is not exactly easy for organizations (as opposed to individual employees) to be philosophical. Typically, in a Tester organization, you will find what Nassim Taleb calls a barbell organizational strategy: a strong focus on metaphysical values and manifestos on one end, paired with a strong focus on data-driven skepticism and interrogation on the other. There low patience for high-concept middleware between those two extremes. Within tester organizations, you will find habits of challenging and interrogating claims and data, strong belief in instrumentation and monitoring of operations, and a non-ironic, non-theatrical continuous dialogue around foundational values and principles. There will often be a culture of ritual adversarial thinking within. They believe they are *rational* organizations.

Of course, depending on how much they are actually winning or losing, the organizational self-images may be more or less deluded in different ways. That's where people like us come in, and where management jokes are born, but that's a story for another day.

The market sizes represented by these four kinds of organizations for consulting services are hard to determine. I suspect, in terms of sheer population size, Achiever organizations are the most common. I'd guess as high as 70%, followed by Integrator, Explorer, and Tester organizations.

The raw population statistics however, are misleading, since the actual market size needs to be weighted by:

- the relative sizes of the organizations (revenue/market cap for private sector; operating budgets for government/non-profit)
- profitability, which determines the discretionary funding available for hiring consulting support
- sectoral culture around hiring external consulting support *vs.* relying on building out internal resources and capabilities.

For example, even though the Tester type organization is probably the rarest, the big tech companies are almost all Tester, tend to have tons of discretionary cash, but are almost always systematically averse to using that money to hire consultants (which makes getting hired by one of them a bit of a coup), relative to old economy organizations. They all love contractors though.

At the other extreme, individual government agencies at any level usually have very little *discretionary* money, but due to sheer scale there's a lot in aggregate. But you have to navigate layers of bureaucratic defenses and processes to get at any of it. To the point that there are meta-consultants who specialize in teaching small businesses and other consultants how to sell to the government.

YOUR CONSULTING STYLE

To determine your consulting style, ask yourself what is the *easiest* kind of deal for you to close, ideally via inbound leads. Do you find it easiest to convince an HR person to sponsor a training workshop on a particular skill, or do individual senior executives tend to reach out to you for a particular personalized need based on your blog posts?

I personally operate almost entirely in the top right quadrant, and almost entirely serving individual senior executives who reach out to me, rather than their organizations. The organizations I have worked with so far have been a more mixed bag. I've worked with organizations of each of the four types.

The reason for the difference is subtle and worth understanding even if you typically serve one of the other quadrants. In general, the higher up in the organization your primary individual client or internal champion, the more their individual personality will override the organization's personality. An Explorer type middle-manager in an HR department within an overall Achiever organization is unlikely to have the influence to find the budget to hire you for a scenarios-and-futures workshop. But an Explorer type Senior VP can pull it off, even if it goes against the organizational grain.

Also note a subtlety: outside and inside are relative. An outer world problem for an executive can be an inner world problem for the organization, and how you operate depends on the role you've been cast into in the drama: working for the organization as a whole, or for the organization as seen from the perspective of a particular executive.

If you find it easiest to sell to middle managers, your style is determined by the typical organization type you sell into, and the individuals you end up working with will be a mixed bag.

If you find it easiest to sell to senior executives or individual clients, your style is determined by the specific individuals who tend to hire you, and the organizations you work with will be a mixed bag.

Take a shot at plotting yourself along both dimensions of the 2x2. Here's my self-assessment: Along the *confidence/doubt dimension*, I'm so bad at serving people and organizations looking for systematic confidence, if I could reliably detect them up front, I'd run away every time. Along the *inner/outer dimension*, I'm generally better at outer-world locus consulting than inner-world. It's not that I'm uninterested in others' inner lives; I'm just uninterested/ill-equipped to help with the doubt/confidence dimension of inner life, which is where most people need the help. Note that the same person or organization may have needs (and the money to pay for support in) all four quadrants. When I started in 2011, I was surprised by the percentage of clients who *also* hired people in other quadrants. Now I expect it. Some spend thousands of dollars a month on an entire support suite. Relying on external consulting support is an operational orientation. That said, the client's personality generally favors one or the other of the quadrants, especially for individuals.

CLASSIFYING YOUR CLIENT

How can you tell which kind of potential client you are looking at? Here's a handy set of tells that work both at individual and organizational levels, *mutatis mutandis*.

The tell of the *Explorer in Need* is a sense of staleness and being in a rut evident in ways of talking, distractibility, and arbitrary pursuit of Next Shiny New Things. The situation needs a dose of freshness and a shake-up of perspectives, and they know it, but don't quite know how to address it.

The tell of the *Achiever in Need* is energy being dissipated in *random acts of X* where they are thrashing and improvising behaviors in an area where skilled and disciplined behavioral precedents exist. Marketing is a function that is particularly prone to this.

The tell of the *Integrator in Need* is endemic mental health issues across activities. There is too much anxiety. There are communication problems everywhere. Relationships are fraying all over the place. Morale is plummeting.

The tell of the *Tester in Need* is toxic arguments that go nowhere, disagreements over facts and data that get weaponized along lines of control, big ego conflicts, and ideological battles. Behaviors are driven more by the need to feed ongoing beefs than accomplish missions. Monitoring, instrumentation, and data governance are heavily politicized. Notice something? In each case, you classify the organization by looking for a locus of futile energy expenditure. That futility is your opportunity.

An important point to keep in mind, incidentally, is that both individuals and organizations can have two polar opposite reasons for hiring a consultant: to build on a strength or to mitigate a weakness. And it might surprise you to hear this, but it is vastly more common for both individuals and organizations to be driven by a growth motivation (working on strengths) in retaining consulting support. It usually takes a crisis situation to drive an individual or organization to seek external help for a weakness. The *crisis gig* economy is a whole distinct economy in its own right.

In each of the four cases, and whether the motive is growth-oriented or deficiency-oriented, the way the consultant addresses both the symptoms and root causes is by injecting a much-needed dose of disinterested systematicity in the right place.

3

A TALE OF TWO SCHOOLS
THERE IS A WAR BREWING AND YOU'VE ALREADY PICKED A SIDE

A FAULT LINE that runs through the consulting world. You can find it in every corner, from Fortune 100 strategy work and function-specific work to startup-whispering and boutique design agency work. You can even find it far from big organizations in domains like life coaching for stay-at-home housewives.

The fault line is live. It seems to propagate through completely new consulting domains as fast as they emerge. This is the divide between the *Positioning* and *People* schools of consulting. The essential difference between the two schools is that the Positioning school takes its intellectual cues from economics and uses formal models and numbers as the ultimate foundation for everything, while the People school takes its intellectual cues from sociology and psychology and uses narrative as the ultimate foundation for everything. If you think these big-picture schisms only matter at C-suite levels, for billion-dollar problems, think again. A life coach might adopt a spreadsheet-driven life optimization approach (this essay[1] explains how you can do that) or one that looks more like psychoanalysis. Or take the newish field of crypto. The Bitcoin world is already exhibiting Positional school biases, while the Ethereum world is already exhibiting People school biases.

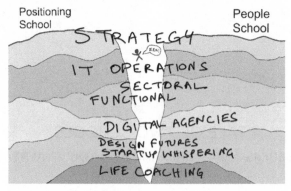

| *Positioning* and *People* schools of consulting

WHY SHOULD YOU CARE?

You should care because a great deal of energy has been building up along this fault line ever since the internet matured as an economic medium around 2000, destabilizing a 50-year-old detente between these two schools. A detente that favored the Positioning school.

A war of ideas is coming, and you're going to get caught up in it one way or another.

You should also care because indie consulting is almost entirely People school. The converse is also true, though less strongly so: the People school is dominated by indie consultants (and smaller boutique agencies). So merely by identifying as a current or aspiring indie consultant, chances are, you're at least unconsciously sympathetic to the governing philosophies of the People school, and unsympathetic to those of the Positioning school. This means you've likely already picked a side, and it's probably the People side.

Walter Kiechel's excellent 2010 book, *Lords of Strategy*, has a good account of the history of the Positioning vs. People schism in the strategy consulting world, where the divide is clearest (here's my review[2]), so I won't rehash that. Let's skip right to the methodological differences between the two schools.

THE GREAT PLAYBOOKS

This chapter's application of the Bohr principle from the first chapter: *the opposite of every Great Playbook is also a Great Playbook.* The Positioning school tries to operate by this Great Playbook:

1. Assume a relatively simple, predictable model of the players in a situation (example, rational actors, bounded rational actors, or legibility-biased rational actors).
2. Make a standardized, relatively detailed, and data-driven map of the environment.
3. Place the simplified people models on the map.
4. Simulate possible futures, pick the best ones, and then use the player models to prescribe courses of action.
5. "Execute" the solution and monitor the evolution of the situation with a feedback loop.

The People school tries to operate by this Great Playbook:

1. Take an inventory of actual named players in the situation, sorting them into rings by their level of agency and ability to influence the situation.
2. Make up a story to account for the recent history of the situation, using abductive reasoning[3], to uncover what the actual players are up to, and why.
3. Start "nudging" the situation to test your narrative, and start forming live, evolving judgments about the actual players: who matters, who doesn't, how they align/don't align, what futures they are working towards.
4. Pick the group of players you think is both *right* about the future, and capable of *winning* the future. Help them win. If such a group doesn't exist, or you're on the wrong side, exit the situation or switch sides.

5. Keep retelling the story and nudging the action according to the current narrative logic, monitoring the evolving situation for narrative violations and disruptions.

Of course, these are just broad predispositions. In practice, both schools muddy their own idealized playbooks a lot. Still, there is something like a grain to how problems get analyzed and solved by the two schools, an overall tendency.

My playbook caricatures attempt to capture those dispositions and tendencies visible under actual case histories. The reason there is usually a clear tendency one way or the other is that opposed Great Playbooks are based on opposed Great Truths, and people tend to swing towards one or the other:

The Great Truth of the Positioning school is that objective, external reality is everything and subjective reality is just noise that gets in the way, but is easily tuned out.

The Great Truth of the People school is that subjective, internal realities (note the plural) are everything and objective reality is a matter of evolving consensus and dissensus.

The resulting methodological divide between the schools is pretty unmistakable.

THE METHODOLOGICAL DIVIDE

For the Positioning school, narratives, if used at all, are a matter of cosmetics and optics. A way to package, present, and influence using the conclusions of a one-size-fits-all playbook.

Positioning school practitioners are essentially wonks at heart, who believe in truth-by-spreadsheet, but sometimes make what they think of as concessions to human nature by telling stories.

For the People school, formal models and data, if used at all, are like specialized forensic investigative tools to be used when the process of repeatedly retelling the story while nudging it along runs into show-stopping mysteries and puzzles. People school practitioners are essentially storytellers at heart, who believe in truth-by-narrative, but sometimes make what they think of as concessions to empiricist insecurities by including data and graphs.

These two Great Playbooks are in an eternal cosmic dance with each other. It should be obvious that the former produces scalable, generalizable, somewhat universal solution templates for widespread problems, while the latter produces non-scalable, bespoke, hard-to-generalize solutions for specific situations.

PEAK POSITIONING SCHOOL

Great Truths are eternal and unfalsifiable. Great Playbooks never go away, they are simply rewritten for new eras through cycles of prominence and obscurity.

That doesn't mean that all Great Truths are equally true at all times. When a Great Truth and its associated Great Playbook get too powerful, internal contradictions start to blow up. Then you get a collapse and recession, during which the opposed Great Truth rises from its own recession. So you have two yin-yang cycles of peaks and troughs.

The Positioning school has been on the ascendant for about 400 years, with a particularly rapid rise to near-total dominance in the second half of the 20th century. The People school, on the other hand, has been in recession for nearly as long and is due for a resurgence.

Peak Positioning was probably sometime between 2001 and 2015. The output of the Positioning school has declined in quality if not quantity. It hasn't had truly fresh big ideas to offer since the late 90s and is running largely on momentum and fumes at this point.

THE LAY OF THE LAND

By my estimate, about 80% of the consulting industry (in terms of revenue and profits, but not headcount) is aligned formally or informally with the Positioning school. It comprises relatively larger firms and institutions, including the Big Three consulting firms (McKinsey, Bain, BCG), the Romulan Empire, and Mordor. It scales all the way down to firms of a couple of hundred. Many indie consultants who are alums of larger organizations also run the Positioning school playbook.

The heart of the Positioning world is Harvard Business School and the Pope of sorts is Michael Porter. Other leading intellectuals of the Positioning school include Emperor Palpatine and Saruman. Institutionally, it is organized as what Kiechel calls a literary-industrial complex, comprising prestigious publications, conferences, and a busy book-producing cottage industry to document the never-ending stream of structuralist models of the world. Positioning school people wear expensive suits and fly around in business class.

The People school is much more of a fragmented grab-bag world of small firms and indie consultants. Instead of a single heart, it has a distributed presence all over the world, with small, volunteer-staffed outposts in Silicon Valley, the University of Toronto, and Tatooine. Instead of a Pope, it has dozens of contending thought leaders, such as Karl Weick, Gareth Morgan, Albus Dumbledore, Yoda, Sun Tzu, and Lao Tze.

Though we have occasionally had a few of our people at Positioning school strongholds, such as the late Clay Christensen at Harvard, institutionally the People school comprises a shadowy network of personal relationships, and a vast, hidden warren of email lists, slacks, Twitter conversations, and messaging groups. We typically wear Henleys, rarely fly business class, and often orienteer cross-country to get from Point A to Point B. Instead of a literary-industrial complex, we have something more like a background tradition of evolving oral history with many more contending ideas and no clear canon at the core. To quote from my review of Kiechel's book:

> [*Lords of Strategy*] quotes one study which found that 105 experts polled for "key ideas" from the [People] school produced 146 candidates, of which 106 were unique. With that much dissent, the "People" school doesn't stand a chance in the commercial marketplace for retail business ideas (which is why, by my reasoning, it is automatically more valuable, since fewer people understand the ideas). By contrast, in the "Positioning" school, there are perhaps a couple of dozen key ideas that everybody agrees are important, which every MBA student learns, and most non-MBA managers eventually learn through osmosis.

I wrote that in 2010, when the tide was just starting to turn in favor of the People school (which Kiechel notes in his book). Springtime is coming for the People school, and winter for the Positioning school. So congrats, you picked the right side at the right time. Be wary though, of getting all tribal about it. Being a consultant is about staying in a state of dynamic balance, evolving your own game with the shifting balance of power between Great Truths and Great Playbooks.

The Positioning school may be headed for an extended recession, but there will still be times when its Great Truth will prevail. The People school may be ascendant and headed for dominance in the post-digital world, but there will still be times when its Great Truth will fail. Think of this as the difference between riding a bicycle and sailing a sailboat. A bicycle in a state of balance is upright except when taking corners. But a sailboat might lean strongly in one direction or the other, depending on the direction of the prevailing wind and the direction you need to go.

As this war of ideas unfolds, you want to be a sailboat, not a bicycle.

---

1. www.mcsweeneys.net/articles/my-fully-optimized-life-allows-me-ample-time-to-optimize-yours
2. www.ribbonfarm.com/2010/05/04/the-lords-of-strategy-by-walter-kiechel/
3. www.ribbonfarm.com/2016/09/07/startups-secrets-and-abductive-reasoning/

4

KNOWING WHICH NUT TO TIGHTEN

CONSULTING AND THE PRINCIPAL-AGENT PROBLEM

THERE'S a joke I like that illustrates the foundational role of knowledge in consulting work:

Guy takes his car to the mechanic because it is making a mysterious noise. Mechanic opens up the hood and tightens one nut. Mysterious noise gone!

"That'll be $50," says the mechanic.

"Hey!" the customer protests, "All you did was tighten one nut! How is that $50?"

"Let me print out an itemized bill for you," says the mechanic. The itemized bill:

YAK AUTO REPAIR	
TIGHTEN NUT	$ 0.10
KNOW WHICH NUT TO TIGHTEN	$49.90
TOTAL	$50.00

Knowing which nut to tighten to resolve a mysterious noise is a simple example of a *knowledge asymmetry*. In this case, the knowledge was everything. The mechanic didn't bring any execution skills to the party. He could have *consulted* on which nut to tighten for $49.90 and the customer could have done the *execution* themselves, saving $0.10.

This is often the case in consulting. The execution skill is often either trivial or available in-house in the client organization. The entire value lies in knowing which nut to tighten.

KNOWLEDGE ASYMMETRIES

The joke illustrates two features of knowledge asymmetries. On the one hand, it highlights the *value* of knowledge asymmetries. Knowing which nut to tighten is in a sense priceless. Somebody who does not know which nut to tighten will waste hours trying to figure it out, and possibly do dumb things that make the problem irreversibly worse. In the worst case, the cost of the unfixed loose-nut problem might be the whole car being lost in an accident, possibly with loss of life.

But it would be a general waste of cognitive resources if everybody knew enough about cars to solve the loose-nut problem, which might occur in one out of a hundred cars over its lifetime. It makes sense for a few specialists—preferably people who have self-selected into car repair because they like the work—to know about the mysterious-noise/loose-nut connection and do the nut-tightening for everybody.

On the other hand, the joke also illustrates the obvious potential for abuse, hinted at in the opaque "knowing which nut to tighten" claim. The mechanic could easily have screwed around doing nothing for hours or even days, made needless repairs with expensive parts, and finally done the nut-tightening as well. The customer wouldn't have been any the wiser. Worse, even if the mechanic doesn't do that, how does the customer know that $49.90 is an appropriate price for the "knowing"? Would other mechanics charge the same? Was the knowing the result of something you might learn in a weekend auto-repair course, or the result of 30 years of experience and pattern-recognition training? Is it a reasonable markup on amortized learning costs? Or rent-seeking?

These problems, of course, are aspects of the famous *principal-agent problem.*[1] While it is inherent to all knowledge work, the principal-agent problem is particularly acute in any relationship where the typical principal has a need that is rare enough that there is no incentive for them to get systematically knowledgeable about the domain, while fulfilling the need is so common an activity for the agent that they have incentives to learn to do it very cheaply, systematically, and efficiently.

A personal example: my sparring-conversation model maps to a type of conversation I tend to have once every week or two with a different client. So I get 25–50 practice sessions a year. But some of my lower-frequency clients (often C-level execs at mid-size companies who have to do all the high-level thinking for their companies on their own) tell me that I'm the only one they have such conversations with, so their frequency is perhaps 1–2 times a year.

KNOWLEDGE ASYMMETRIES FOR EMPLOYEES

The principal-agent problem does affect regular employer-employee relationships, but is not as severe for several reasons.

- A manager—the internal "customer" for the work of an employee—is likely to have *done* the same kind of work before being tapped to supervise it.
- The relationship is longer-term and higher frequency. It is harder to hide the nature of a problem when an instance is being detected and solved every week.

- There are likely peers with the same kind of knowledge, and strong incentives to rat out a fellow employee who is exploiting principal-agent knowledge asymmetries.
- Much of the asymmetric knowledge is actually in proprietary systems rather than in the heads of particular employees.

As a result of these factors, in work done by employees there is a visible, reasonable-seeming correlation between effort and problems. And in general, the more important the problem is judged to be, the greater the cost of the effort. This is not an accident. It is practically the definition of an organization: a collection of systematically monitored, high-frequency activities defined by reasonable-seeming correlations between effort and output. In fact, you could argue that the core competency of organizations is knowing —at a codified process level—how much effort it *should* take to accomplish any of a vast array of core activities they can do better than outsiders, and setting appropriate compensation policies.

If you're one of those people who like to analyze firms in terms of Coasean transaction costs,[2] this effect can be seen as lower *monitoring* costs in a relationship. An employee is simply cheaper for an organization to monitor for dishonesty or ineffectiveness than an infrequently used consultant. A much-worse-than-average employee (in terms of either dishonesty or incompetence) will soon be spotted.

A genius employee, who routinely finds 1-minute solutions to problems that take peers days, will either be promoted to work on the hardest problems, or have their thinking skills analyzed and turned into teachable disciplines or automated support systems for non-genius employees. They are likely to turn into teachers themselves, trading the asymmetric knowledge for esteem.

The net effect of these two feedback loops is that behaviors that do not exhibit a reasonable-seeming correlation between effort and output either get weeded out or tweaked until they do.

What's more, this dynamic also makes it harder for the firm itself to be dishonest the larger it gets, because more people with agent-side participation in knowledge asymmetries have to collude (so a tell of a possibly shady firm is a great deal of internal secrecy between groups that minimizes the number of people with complicity in any given deception).

Any employee with a very unique, opaque, and illegible skill is a huge risk for an organization. To prevent such an employee from falling prey to principal-agent temptations, or being poached by a competitor, they are likely to end up so highly compensated that it is simply not worth their time or energy to exploit the asymmetries of their knowledge. Often a uniquely skilled but underutilized employee, despite being compensated enough to make dishonesty uninteresting, will end up leaving and becoming a consultant simply to find more things to do.

REASONABLE EFFORTS FOR REASONABLE OUTPUT

I've used the relative phrase *reasonable-seeming* rather than the absolute *reasonable* to describe the perception of effort in tasks done by employees. Therein lies a subtlety. The work of an organization is a theater of apparent reasonableness that may or may not be actually reasonable, depending on whether or not the foundational assumptions of the internal reality of an organization are actually true.

Quite often, these assumptions are at least slightly out-of-date. Often, they are wildly, insanely obsolete, in ways that are obvious to outsiders. Internally though, the organization may be unconsciously pumping a massive amount of energy into denying what's obvious to outsiders. It may take serious social courage to challenge the "consensus of reasonableness" in the internal economy of valuing efforts and outcomes. On the other hand, outsiders can be very, very wrong in interpreting the externally visible behaviors of an organization, in which case reasonable-seeming is actually reasonable in an absolute sense, and it is the world outside that is insane in its beliefs about what "reasonable" looks like. In some cases, there is no way to easily tell whether the organization is deluded or the external world is deluded. The best you can do is think hard about it (from either side of the organization's boundary) and wait for the judgment of history. In either case though, one of the tells of an organization working very hard to stabilize a dissonance between internal and external realities is *resistance to consultants*:

> When the internal reality is deluded, consultants might inject an entirely unwelcome reality check.

> When external reality is deluded, consultants might contaminate a fragile island of deeper truth by injecting bad external thinking.

In either case, we consultants represent informational risks and threats to the organizations we try to help and it's generally up to us to manage the risk.

NEUTRALIZING YOUR RISKS

This entire system breaks down in areas where the organization does *not* know enough to efficiently deploy as employee knowledge, but has a strong (possibly rational) resistance to plugging knowledge gaps using consultants. Consulting begins where monitoring costs get too high, relative to need frequency, for employees to be the right answer. That doesn't mean the monitoring cost problem goes away. It tends to get solved in varied ways:

1. Crisis-only consulting policies: Organizations will simply resist retaining consulting services unless there is a crisis, and the costs of not bringing in outside expertise

to help become unacceptable. These organizations simply leave certain knowledge-gap risks unmanaged.

2. Ecosystem competency: Organizations will consciously develop competency in managing an ecosystem of consultants via specialized monitoring mechanisms— think certification programs.

3. Externalize the risk explicitly: Many organizations will require consultants and contractors to carry specialized insurance policies, as some of you will know. I've never yet taken such a gig.

4. Relying on exceptions: Many organizations will have default no-consultant policies, but allow senior executives to make exceptions based on special needs, and the existence of trusted relationships. This of course, is an entry point for a lot of cronyism.

In my experience, the most common approach is the first one, leaving non-crisis knowledge gap risks unmanaged. Approach 2 works where there is a skills base that the organization can control and shape in some way (such as by owning the core design of a product). Approach 3 passes the buck to the consultant.

In the previous chapter, *A Tale of Two Schools*, I took some cheap shots at the economics-inspired Positioning school of consulting. Here I've tried to give you a glimpse of how an economics lens can sometimes be useful in understanding how to approach gigwork. The conclusion to draw from this, however, is that your best approach to creating trust and getting good gigs is Approach 4, i.e., a People-school approach to a problem whose structure is illuminated by a Positioning-school analysis.

Build relationships that allow you to be an exception to anti-consultant rules/barriers. So long as you keep yourself honest by resisting the lure of cronyism, and only taking gigs where it is clear that you're bringing genuine external knowledge or relationships to the party, it is the best way to address the legitimate principal-agent concerns of clients, without bearing too heavy a burden of externalized risk-management costs yourself.

_____

1. en.wikipedia.org/wiki/Principal%E2%80%93agent_problem
2. en.wikipedia.org/wiki/Transaction_cost

5

YOU ARE NOT A SCIENTIST

GIGUPS AND STARTUPS SHARE AN IMPORTANT ATTRIBUTE: NEITHER IS SCIENCE-BASED

IN 2012, I did a talk about the startup psyche titled *Should You Drink the Kool-Aid?* The 2x2 on the next page is the core graphic of that talk, transposed from the startup key to the indie consulting key. It is meant to help you think about a very important question: *how do you know the core things you think you know?*

This is a central question for us students of the art of gig. Indie consultants need to be aware of their operating epistemology, in order to avoid buying their own bullshit, and turning into unconscious grifters.

STARTUPS AND GIGUPS

It is no coincidence that a 2x2 from a talk about startups is easy and useful to transpose to a discussion of indie consulting. The two domains are so similar it can be hard to keep them apart in your head. In particular, startup knowledge *also* revolves around the same question. In both cases, the answer is the same: *how do you know the core things you know? Definitely not in a scientific way!*

Beyond the obvious surface-level similarities—small scale, financial precarity, cash-flow volatility—both startups and what we might call gigups share a deep feature: their associated modes of knowing are not science. Whatever the shared epistemology of gigology and startupology, it isn't a scientific one.

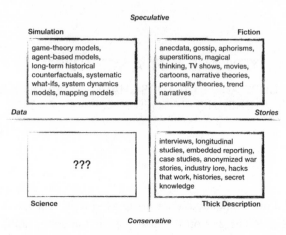

| The Four Modes of Consulting Knowledge

If you're an entrepreneur or an indie consultant, whatever else you might be, you are not a scientist. You may use or do some science along the way, but it will be peripheral to your core way of knowing. And crucially, if you want to succeed, you'll find you can't stop at the science. There is no such thing as an evidence-based startup or gigup. In the world of gigups and startups, only failures can be evidence-based.

The core of your real work begins where the science ends. A strictly scientific self-image is self-limiting for an indie consultant. To look for the secret sauce of an indie consulting offering *only* where the light of science can shine is to act like the drunk in the parable, looking for his keys where the street light is shining rather than wherever in the dark he dropped them. This does not mean the native modes of knowing in gigups are illegitimate or useless. In fact, thinking that, developing science envy, and trying to put a scientific gloss on non-scientific modes of knowing, is the surest way of destroying the kinds of legitimate value they do produce. The 2x2 captures three possible good answers to the question *how do you know the important things you think you know?*Through fiction, through simulation, and through thick description (a fancy word for anthropology). None of these is science, but all of them are valuable modes of knowing.

Science, loosely speaking, is a conservative, data-driven mode of knowing. Indie consulting is speculative and/or story-driven. The *science* quadrant of the 2x2 is *???* because there is in a sense nothing there that can be a core part of what you know as an indie consultant. This took me a few years to realize. In the original version of the 2x2 I had some stuff in that quadrant that I was giving the benefit of doubt and labeling "science." Now I'm convinced there is no there there, just people performing various forms of science theater. If there is science to it, it is not part of your core. If it is part of your core, it isn't science. If it's a real science, there will be pure scientists working adjacent to whatever you're doing (setting aside the parlor game of "who is the real scientist") to whom your use of their output will seem like a profane "application." When it comes to gigups and startups, nothing important that you think you know is known in a scientific sense. In the process of going from . . .

The ball bounces this way because physics.

. . . to . . .

Calculating how the ball bounces is valuable for Great Yak Enterprises because *x*.

. . . you inevitably, and inexorably, go from science to something else. Whatever that is, to call it *science* is a distortion of it, and a disservice to it. But in that *X* lies the core of how you *do* know things and add value.

THE PRICE OF INTEGRATION

Why is science lost in going from pure bouncing balls to applied bouncing balls? What is gained in giving up a purely scientific posture in what you're doing? In the simplest terms, science is "lost" because startups and gigups both require integrative modes of knowing, and the price of achieving effective integration is that you must necessarily go beyond the limits of scientific modes of knowing.

This may be a cliché, but science is reductionist by design, and this is both a good thing and the strength of the scientific mode of knowing. You take an ambiguous phenomenon, and carve out a piece about which you can make relatively unambiguous assertions. The reduction is not a bug or flaw: it is what makes ambiguity reduction possible at all. Ambiguity reduction is the *point* of carving out a piece to work with.

When you try to "science" a system, you don't carve out pieces that are important, interesting, or useful. Those are merely nice-to-have features you can hope for in a carved-out piece, but essentially unrelated to whether or not you can science it well. The chances that you can "carve reality at the joints" in ways that conform to the contours of practical concerns are low.

You carve out a part that offers potential for systematic ambiguity reduction, and *hope* that when you go back (*if* you can go back) and integrate it into an understanding of the whole, some of that lowered ambiguity will pay dividends in some unpredictable way. To bring science to a party is to take a leap of faith that you'll be able to go from holistic to reductionist and then back to holistic. But being able to go back is not guaranteed. It's a bit like killing yourself, hoping to be resurrected in a stronger form.

Simulation, storytelling, and thick descriptions are integrative modes of knowing. When you've taken something apart and scienced what you can science (and that subset might be "nothing"), the real work of a startup or gigup begins.

6

THE FOUR RESPONSE REGIMES
OF CONSULTING

WHAT MIX OF RISK AND TIME PRESSURE DO YOU
HELP YOUR CLIENTS RESPOND TO?

I CAME up with a model of four regimes of consulting, illustrated in the 2x2 on the next page, while trying to figure out why my response to a family emergency seemed inadequate, even by my own mediocre-slacker standards. I concluded that what I deal with poorly is the combination of *high risk* and *high time pressure*.

These seemed like good axes for thinking about regimes of indie consulting as well, so I figured I'd explore the time-pressure vs. risk 2x2. It is a cousin of the well-known important vs. urgent 2x2 (the Eisenhower matrix, popularized by Stephen Covey), but the shifts in variables helped me think more clearly about *response* regimes in particular.

Viewed from a time-pressure/risk perspective, the roles of consultants of all types can be understood as participation in non-routine institutional response patterns. Some of these response capabilities are available as on-demand services from another large firm that has aggregated enough demand to smooth out variability and sustain a separate corporate existence, but this is obviously not for us indie consultants.

So where do we indie consultants fit? We help address capa-

bility shortfalls that fall through the cracks between in-house capabilities and systematically outsourceable capabilities. Indie
consultants naturally fit in where the capability gap is either small
enough and oddly-shaped enough to be filled by a few individually
contracted people, *or* where the gap is large, but can be filled by a
fairly generic type of labor without the help of a labor-aggregating
counterparty.

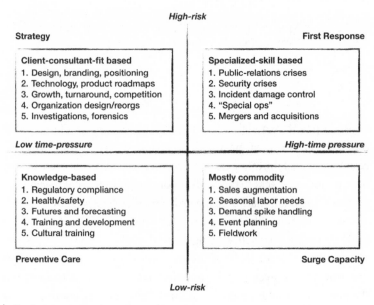

The four response regimes of consulting

EXTRA-INSTITUTIONAL RESPONSE PATTERNS

Earlier, in *Elements of Consulting Style*, I outlined four styles based
on four types of clients. This response regimes 2x2 gives you an
alternative set of four styles, based on four types of situational
response you might be helping clients craft.

If you apply both 2x2s to what you do, you'll likely end up with
a good triangulation of who you are as an indie consultant. Your

offering might fall into any of the sixteen types suggested by the two 2x2s. For instance, I offer *Strategy for Explorers*. You might be in *Preventive Care for Integrators* or *Surge Capacity for Testers*. Here's a handy 4x4 table for you to think about. Try classifying the gigs you've done or would like to do on it.

		Client type			
		Explorer	Achiever	Integrator	Tester
Response regimes	**Strategy**				
	Preventive Care				
	Surge Capacity				
	First Response				

| *Classifying gigs*

Indie consultants help client companies generate responses to events and situations for which they lack an internal capacity, and which they do not understand in a systematic-enough way to outsource to another large company (indeed, aggregator service providers may not even exist in sufficiently messy and treacherous capability minefields). In other words, indie consultants are part of *extra-institutional* response patterns. That much is obvious.

What is perhaps less obvious is that the lack of systematized capability (either in-house or outsourced) is generally rational. Perhaps the need arises infrequently or unpredictably. Or perhaps

it is a one-and-done deal like logo design. Or perhaps there is a
supply glut, making it easy for companies to hire what they need
when they need it. Curiously, many struggling consultants seem to
believe that the lack of in-house capacity for the services they offer
is irrational. That their work ought to be a job and that they ought
to be hired as an employee to do it. This belief leads to weird and
potentially crippling mental blocks that put you in the worst of
both worlds.

Let's survey the four types of extra-institutional response:
preventative care, surge capacity, strategy, and first response.

PREVENTIVE CARE

The low-risk, low time-pressure quadrant is a very crowded (for
obvious reasons) and demand-limited market. It is also something
of a lemon market: bad actors driving out the good. It is easy to
convince yourself—and certain kinds of gullible clients with more
budget than sense—that many preventive-care consulting products
and services are necessary. This is the kind of consulting offering
(often made up by laid-off mid-career middle managers who have
succumbed to up-or-out pressures) that best fits the accusation that
consultants are people who help solve problems that wouldn't exist
in the first place without them.

Preventive care is usually a knowledge-based consulting offering. The main principled question to ask is whether the knowledge is useful or necessary for the client. If you have to struggle
to sell the value of the knowledge and it feels like lecturing
someone without teeth to floss regularly, you might want to
reflect on how necessary the knowledge you're hawking is.You
might want to ask yourself honestly what the actual risks and
costs of ignoring the knowledge (and you as the bearer of it) are
for the client and why they seem to be getting along fine without
it. Perhaps your prospective clients are not quite as dumb as you
think for turning down your proposal for a two-million-dollar

all-hands 12-Step Alien Attack Preparedness workshop (box lunch included).

SURGE CAPACITY

The high-time-pressure/low-risk quadrant is the commodity quadrant of consulting. If consultants are being hired in job lots, driven largely by predictable or unpredictable demand spikes affecting the client, it is surge capacity. If you feel like part of an *Uber for X* workforce hanging around hoping for surge pricing to kick in, you might be in this quadrant.

If you're in this quadrant, chances are you'll struggle to brand and position yourself uniquely. You'll also struggle to set your own price or differentiate yourself from contract labor supplied by contracting companies. One test: you have a blog, portfolio site, or other marketing asset, but most of your work still comes through gig sites like Upwork. You're unable to actually attract any work at your preferred bill rate, and are forced to work at prevailing market rates.

Note that the low-risk part is at the individual level. For a company that needs to temporarily double its sales force to exploit a seasonal demand surge, the opportunity costs of missing the big selling window overall may be huge, so in aggregate, the response may be a high-risk one. But retaining a given *individual* consultant is not a high-risk move, since there are many participating in the response, and any individual consultant is dispensable/easily replaced.

STRATEGY

This quadrant is generally where I hang out, though I make the occasional foray into the preventive-care quadrant. High risk and low time pressure is generally the combination of conditions that makes anything *strategic*. Things that end up in this quadrant are generally the most thinky types of consulting offerings, but surprisingly (and unlike the preventive-care quadrant) are not strongly knowledge- or skill-based. Instead, they are based on client-consultant fit and trust.

Strategy-centric offerings are usually based on a track record that induces trust, and idiosyncratic personal mind-melds of taste and intellectual style between client and consultant. Since there are no skills *per se*, beyond general intelligence, and there is generally enough time to read and research relevant information, knowledge matters less than the ability to connect with the client's capability shortfall in an effective and trustworthy way.

A good strategy consultant is often simply someone who is good at just being present in a situation without becoming yet another part of the problem. This can be surprisingly hard to do. Many a time I've watched "strategy" people walk into a messy situation and pick out, with unerring accuracy, the role to occupy that makes them the biggest new piece of the problem.

Sometimes, all I do in a situation is listen and bear witness to whatever is going on, occasionally drawing attention to this or that piece of the puzzle, adding nothing new. I've received the most appreciation when I manage to do that well. It's kinda fun working in a zone where "great, you didn't make it worse!" is rare enough to be appreciated.

FIRST RESPONSE

This is the quadrant that I'd probably be worst at, if I tried to operate in it. I'd put stuff like security or PR crises there. The combination of high risk and high time pressure implies that it is a zone where there is no time to learn or even translate knowledge into actions via deliberate analysis.

You have to be able to pattern-match and generate appropriate responses much faster. Not just that, you have to be good at dealing with clients in *abnormal* states, like patients in ICUs. Their ongoing behavior may be shock- or stress-driven, and be entirely inappropriate and unskilled. Their regular functioning may be severely compromised by the situation. They may be a big part of their own problem. The situation may involve various other parties who have become involved, like law enforcement, disaster relief, or the media. Deep emotional reserves may be necessary for effectiveness.

SECTION TWO

SEEING LIKE AN INDIE

Where you stand depends on where you sit.

RUFUS MILES

7

THE CLUTCH CLASS

GIG WORKERS ARE NOT PART OF EITHER CAPITAL OR LABOR

THE CENTRAL POLITICAL question in gigwork is this: *are we gigworkers part of labor or are we part of capital?* For our purposes, *capital* is a loose category that includes the professional managerial class as well as the share-owning class. *Labor* includes anyone for whom incentives suggest collective action as a good general strategic approach to achieving political goals, and whose share of capital ownership is too small to make a difference to their political goals.

So which are we? Capital or labor? The short answer is, we are neither. We constitute a separate emerging political class I call the *clutch* class.

THE NEW CLASS WARS

Around the world, there are battles unfolding over the status of gigworkers. Traditional labor leaders argue that gigworkers, such as rideshare drivers, should be reclassified as regular employees. Opponents (including the companies and many of the workers themselves) argue that most of these workers do not in fact want to be regular employees, since the flexibility of gigwork is what drew them in the first place.

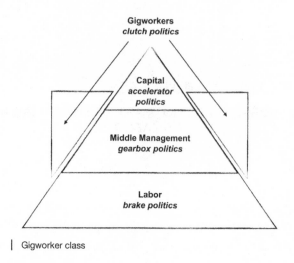

| Gigworker class

Like it or not, a new kind of class warfare is getting started in the economy, and opening moves are being made by both the traditional classes. Given the way politics around the world is shaping up, this war can only heat up in the next few years, not cool down. And the outcome will depend in large part on what we gigworkers decide to do. So where do we gigworkers stand on the matter?

Well, that depends on where we sit.[1]

WHERE WE STAND, WHERE WE SIT

No matter which way you lean in terms of sympathies, there is an objectively correct answer: we are neither labor, nor capital. We are what I think of as the *clutch class*, in two senses of the term.

If you think of organizations as cars, a good mental model of the *politics* (not economics) of work is that capital is the *accelerator*, labor is the *brake*, and middle-management is the *gearbox*. And we gigworkers? We are the *clutch*. We help disengage/re-engage the drivetrain during gear-shifting, as operating regimes change and organizations need to adapt behaviors.

A second sense in which we are the clutch class is in the sense of the sports slang term: we are typically roped in to break stalemates and frustrating equilibriums, and actually make things happen and deliver some high performance during critical periods. Both senses of the word should suggest a very uncomfortable relationship to labor movements and socialist politics.

ARE WE SCABS?

For a true socialist, the harsh view of us gigworkers who actually *like* what we do is that we are a generalized descendent of *scabs.* This perception may or may not bother you (it doesn't bother me), but it's an interesting one to think about. Though we don't always act in ways that are against the interests of the organized labor class, this perception is . . . not wrong.

The defining characteristic of a scab is striking a self-interested *independent* bargain with the capital-owning/managing/leading class that breaks from *any* larger collectively bargained deal. This defection does not have to be from a formal contract between an organized labor union and the managers/owners of a company. Even informal expectations around non-unionized jobs (including high-skill, high-education individual contributor jobs, shaped by an elite culture of norms and conventions) are effectively an emergent collective-bargaining outcome. The interests of individuals are subordinated to those of a larger group through various organic and designed mechanisms. Individuals generally go along with the collective flow, whether or not it's led by union-type structures, and whether or not there are hard or soft coercive forces at work.

For example, around 2010, when wage-limiting collusion was exposed in the tech industry, high-paid techies, not generally given to labor-like sentiments, were as outraged as striking factory workers. And that outrage had an effect even though it wasn't channeled through traditional industrial-action mechanisms. That kind of loose employee activism is becoming increasingly common around all kinds of political issues that affect workplaces.

The defining characteristic of scabs is also the defining feature of the gigworker class. We defect from collective actions and trade-off higher security, better benefits, and lower personal overheads, for two things:

- more personalized working conditions built around needs that may not be shared by any larger group
- continuous, independent maneuvering capability where aligning interests with a group might require too much lock-step marching, or worse, voluntary social immobility.

Why is this often hard for newbie gigworkers to understand? Because we share (especially early on in our careers) many of the practical problems that the most disempowered parts of the laboring economy face: precarity, periods where our income can be worse than minimum wage, health-insurance risks, and few to no social safety net protections unless we pay retail prices out of pocket. But these similarities do not make us part of labor.

HIGH AGENCY, LOW CAPITAL

Though we share some of the problems of labor (and have some uniquely our own, such as a regulatory environment hostile to small/micro business structures), we don't suffer from the same agency limitations in addressing them.

A graphic designer or independent strategy consultant is fundamentally a more mobile type of economic actor than a welder or an auto-assembly specialist. We work with our own cheap tools: laptops and notebooks for the most part, rather than with million-dollar machine tools or billion-dollar factories owned by investors seeking returns. We serve broad rather than narrow patterns of demand.

In the U.S. for instance, a machinist with specialized training in operating a $20 million piece of equipment only used by big airplane manufacturers can pretty much only work within the Boeing or Lockheed Martin ecosystems. A graphic designer not only has a lot more options, but owns their $2,000 set of tools outright. A crane operator can only seek work in large industrial settings operating million-dollar cranes. A Lyft driver can work with their own $25,000 Prius.

It's not that the incentives favoring traditional patterns of collective action in pursuit of political ends are absent, but they are *weak*—too weak to allow for traditional top-down, explicitly organized collective action mechanisms. On the other hand, individual agency is much stronger—much too strong to make coming together in solidarity with "others like me" an obviously smart thing to do.

Why? Because the gig economy, especially the indie consulting corner of it, relies on production capabilities that are 5% based on owned capital equipment and 95% based on affordances of the free internet. The *leverage* of what little capital we own, thanks to the internet, is *enormous*. Bring your own device (BYOD), get your factory for free. So yes, to a 1910s union firebrand, we are no better than traitorous scabs.

But from the perspective of a 2020s digital economy, we are members of the clutch class who largely own our means of production, have too high a degree of agency in shaping our own lives to be part of labor, and too little wealth to be part of capital.

We are in the high-agency/low-capital quadrant of the economy.[2] This makes it worth our while to cut our own deals with whomever we can, whenever we can.

INCENTIVES, NOT MECHANISMS

For a long time, I myself was confused about this. I thought there was a meaningful free agency collective-action mechanism design problem to be solved. I did not recognize that there was a fundamental misalignment of incentives all around, limiting the *desirability* of traditional collective-action mechanisms and outcomes for us gigworkers.

Though I've never personally been in a dire enough situation financially to have to resort to political actions, I've always felt a sympathy towards those who seem to often be in such dire straits. I used to think: *maybe the rag-tag subculture of graphic designers needs a mechanism like the Screen Actors Guild (SAG) to work toward shared interests.*

That was a flawed take. The rare corners of the gig economy where organizing like traditional labor is meaningful—actors are a good example—typically exist where the demand is concentrated enough that it can be targeted by collective action. And Hollywood has, until recently, been a very concentrated industry. Now of course, that political balance of power between big movie studios and the talent market is shifting, thanks to the proliferation of cheap tools for moviemaking. Weird dynamics are being triggered too, perhaps as a result of the changing equilibrium (for example, in 2019, the Screenwriters Guild initiated collective action against the agencies representing them,[3] which is really weird).

With the right talents, you can make an excellent video with an iPhone, upload it to YouTube, raise money on Kickstarter, and make an indie movie on your own, with rented equipment and non-SAG actors. The value of various high-leverage distribution channels like movie theaters is falling by the day. From the point of view of traditionally organized gig labor in Hollywood, I bet this sort of development comes across as a growing scab-like threat to their position. As yet, the threat is not serious, because the big streaming services do need the kind of high-quality content that only Hollywood can currently supply. But that will change, and even Hollywood will turn into collective-action badlands (as an aside, it is weird that 20 years ago, when people first started talking about free agency, the Hollywood Model was often held up as an aspirational ideal; today it is becoming clear that it is an obsolete model to leave behind).

As a thought experiment, consider the challenge of *actually* unionizing in some Union 2.0 form, around whatever it is you do in the gig economy, and think it through a bit. You should get to *reductio ad absurdum* in a few steps.

Take me. As a strategy consultant who works with senior leaders, the very idea of joining up with fellow strategy consultants to form an Independent Strategy Consultants Guild, and trying to establish a defensible collective bargaining position relative to our shared client base—the tens of thousands of senior (typically VP+) executives in the world—sounds silly. If by some absurd miracle such a mechanism came together, your best move would be to scab the hell out of it.

Something about the absurd picture of an ISCG guild president bargaining with a committee of execs in search of consultants just does not compute. Even the basic categories like *president* and *committee* are wrong. This is a not-even-wrong view of how at least this corner of the gig economy works.

And something similar is true of almost every sector where work is organized via the gig economy, one individual contract at a time, one Form 1099 at a time. We are not labor. We are not capital. We are clutch.

We are clutch. We don't waste time in bad equilibria. We either individually help drive discontinuous movements towards better ones or we leave the scene for a better one.

We are clutch. We do not waste time on collective-action political mechanisms. We let individual instincts guide us, and rely on emergent networked dynamics, and the power of exit rather than voice, to drive political change favorable to us.

We are clutch. We do not try to directly compete with capital by accumulating enough of it to be a player on that side. Most of us have lifestyle business goals—make enough to have a good life, but don't kill yourself trying to become a multimillionaire.

Mechanisms do matter, but the ones that we actually employ towards political ends are adapted to *our* political ends, not those of either capital or labor. The medium is the message. For capital, the right mechanisms are based on catalyzing favorable regulations and market mechanisms for capital to seek the highest returns. The message of the medium is growth and acceleration. That's right for them. For labor, the right mechanisms are collective-action based. The message of the medium is stability and security. That's right for them.

For us in the clutch class, with our Slightly Scabby Tendencies, the mechanisms for working towards shared goals are much newer —loose, intelligent coordination around *information advantages.* We swap notes, we share leads, we pitch in to help each other out on specific gigs, we put ourselves in crucible groups to rapidly learn skills far faster than labor or capital, we serve as market makers in an economy of referrals, we do what needs to be done. And we do an end run around the stale battles of the 20th century.

The message of *our* medium is discontinuous change and maneuvering. Not growth for the sake of growth like capitalists, or stability for the sake of stability like labor.

And generally, we are hired by people aligned with the capital class, interested in driving discontinuous change, not by people aligned with the labor class (though there *are* gig economy cottage industries that are labor-aligned and active in certain highly regulated sectors like education and healthcare). That's what makes us scab-like. Whether or not you like that perception.

It's a tough, harsh message for many, since the gig economy is full of people with strongly socialist economic sensibilities, deeply compassionate natures, and values based on solidarity, equality, and social justice, just like the labor class. We do not like to think of our actions as perhaps betraying those values, as embodied by certain older political forms. But I think we are true to those values in deeper, vastly more effective ways.

Push come to shove, where we stand depends on where we sit. And in almost all cases, we sit right next to management and capital, serving as clutch players, helping shift gears where necessary, helping with surge actions, helping break out of stalemates. And where we sit makes us scabs. The burden of that perception is something we have to accept. You're not going to convince a traditional leftie otherwise.

CLUTCH TIME

Let me end on a lighter note (too late you say? well maybe). Labor Day is meant to commemorate the achievements and spotlight the political mission and values of the labor class. Those achievements, that mission, and those values are important, and matter. They should be spotlighted. More power to them. Happy Labor Day to them.

There is no Capital Day because you could argue that every 9-to-5 business day is Capital Day and every big shopping holiday is Mega Capital Day. The mission and values of the capital class are also important, and matter, and should be spotlighted. More power to them. Happy Every Business Day and Happy Black Friday to them. Is there a Clutch Day? A day for us to celebrate ourselves? No, that sort of identity-centric performative class consciousness is for twentieth-century types. The clutch class owns a dark slice of lived *time* rather than a day on the calendar. Clutch Time is evenings and weekends. With apologies to Chris Dixon,[4] what the clutch class does on evenings and weekends, everybody will be doing in ten years.

Clutch time is when capital and labor both try to rest and relax and gigworkers get going. That's the time when those of us in the clutch class really come into our own. We go to meetups, we get coffee with each other. We scan the social streams for openings, seek out room to maneuver, ways to deploy high-leverage cheap assets, learn breakout skills, and dream up hacks and arbitrages. And we sneak one-at-a-time into the future, through gaps on the economic frontier, rather than marching rank-and-file in slogan-chanting cohorts.

We flow like water, shaping the landscape even as we get around it, generally making the stuffy old class hierarchy of the industrial age leak like hell as we flow invisibly through the interstices.

Causing the world to shift gears.

We are not capital.

We are not labor.

We are clutch. And the future belongs to us.

---

1. The reference is to the Rufus Miles quote on the section title page, "Where you stand depends on where you sit," sometimes referred to as Miles' Law.
2. Low agency/low capital is labor; high agency/high capital is capitalist class; low agency/high capital is groups like retirees.
3. variety.com/2019/film/news/writers-guild-agencies-conflict-of-interest-allega tions-1203161563/
4. cdixon.org/2013/03/03/what-the-smartest-people-do-on-the-weekend-is-what-everyone-else-will-do-during-the-week-in-ten-years/

8

INDIE FRAGILITY

INDIE BUSINESSES ARE FRAGILE. COME TO TERMS WITH THAT FACT.

INDIE BUSINESSES ARE *FRAGILE*. *Fragility* is a better framework than *precarity* for us, since it focuses on internal structural things potentially within our control rather than external risks that are not ("precarity" has also become overloaded with political baggage lately, so I'm going to avoid the term).

I can't find statistics for the gig economy, but we're all effectively small businesses, so I'd expect trends to be similar to small businesses in general, and according to the U.S. Small Business Administration, only about 50% of small businesses survive past the fifth year.

I suspect this picture looks far rosier than it actually is. I once met a guy at an airport who specialized in franchise-startup consulting, helping aspiring small business owners choose and set up chain franchise restaurants. He claimed that the survival rate for franchise operators past five years was 70%, but for non-franchise restaurants it was less than 10%. I haven't verified that, but it sounds roughly right, and matches anecdotal evidence I've encountered elsewhere. So small businesses that are effectively part of ecosystems underwritten by larger businesses borrow some robustness from their mother ships, but give up some margin and equity appreciation potential in return.

On the other hand, fragility questions always remind me of Kongō Gumi, which was, for a long time, the oldest continuously running business in the world. It was a small Japanese family firm specializing in Buddhist temple construction. Founded in 578 A.D., it finally shut down in 2006, succumbing to very banal financial hardships of the sort any business might succumb to. It was acquired by a larger company (I doubt the terms were good or commensurate with the brand equity of 1,442 years of operation— distressed businesses are generally sold for pennies on the dollar). Point being, it did not take a Godzilla attack to end the long game for this 1,442-year-old mom-and-pop shop. Just some routine errors that would be recoverable for businesses in good shape.

Both the SBA actuarial statistics and the peculiar longevity and tame ending of exceptions like Kongō Gumi invite analysis. Is the latter an existence proof of an antifragility strategy available to us one-person bands that we might discover, by digging into such cases? Or is it a fooled-by-randomness effect, with examples like Kongō Gumi merely being exceptions that prove the general rule that small businesses are fragile?

FRAGILITY AND SCALE

I personally think the longevity of Kongō Gumi was pure luck. A random data point from an unusually stable business sector in an unusually stable and conservative country. I doubt we could construct a real playbook for business longevity by looking into its history. First-principles analysis would suggest that in general, the smaller a business, the more fragile it is likely to be. And nothing is more fragile than a one-person business operating in the gig economy. A simple bout of the flu can be as devastating for a gigworker as a hurricane for a larger business. I write a subscription newsletter, and I think I have enough earned trust that I wouldn't expect a lot of my paying newsletter readers to unsubscribe if I had to take a week or two off due to illness. But what about three months? Or six? Or a year? I don't think goodwill and concern for my health or financial wellbeing would extend that far. Beyond a point, I'd have to shut the newsletter down, and replace the income with an alternative source that can weather extended illness.

The fragility on the consulting side is even more drastic. One of the things I worry about is: what if I land a big, time-bound gig of say three months that I expect to pay my bills for six months, but then something like a parental health emergency forces me to go be in India for a month, unable to work on the gig? A paycheck employer would likely be understanding and work with me to figure out a revised schedule of work deliverables, or take unpaid time off. A consulting client? I'd expect the gig, especially with a new client, to either evaporate or go to someone else.

These are harsh risks that you must not be in denial about if you are in the gig economy, even if you don't have good solutions to managing them. I certainly don't have good answers. But that's not a good reason to sweep the questions under the rug. This is something I have tried to be conscious of in writing this book. Having been in the game for over a decade, there are certainly some things I understand better than those with less experience, and some risks and challenges I navigate better. But there's a vast universe of uncertainties and risks I understand no better than anyone else. My only advantage on those fronts might be not being in denial about their existence. I've had enough near-misses to lose any false sense of security I might have developed in the wake of the first flush of self-confidence from landing my first couple of gigs.

SMALL IS FRAUGHT

Many lines of business that indies like getting into do not allow for easy scheduling of breaks, interruptions of service, or service-level degradations. *Passive income* is mostly a myth.

Though you are only a single human, you are *seen* as a business, and people expect the kind of reliability and stability they expect of bigger businesses with far greater redundancy in capabilities. This often means indie businesses put themselves under enormous pressure (and take on the resulting health stress) to deliver to expectations set by bigger businesses. That's why you hear of hard-working small business owners, in sectors like cheap restaurants or convenience stores, who haven't taken a day off in years, let alone a vacation. They work to a 24-7-365 SLA and don't have the staffing redundancy to cover for their personal absence.

At the other end of the load-factor spectrum, there is the kind of spiky gigwork where you can make enough in a month or two to pay for an entire year. But then you don't have strong control over the timing of the spike. If the opportunity spike coincides with an emergency spike, you get hit with a double jeopardy: you lose the income opportunity *and* you have to deal with the emergency-related expenses. It's what Charles Perrow labeled a *normal accident*—a condition in a complex system (like nuclear reactors or the modern gig economy tech stack) where two unrelated and ordinary risk events coincide to create extraordinary risk conditions.

This risk was driven home for me in late 2019, when my father-in-law fell seriously ill and passed away. His passing demanded both time (more from my wife than me) to deal with, and significant expenses, over several months. At the time, I had *just* started a year-long fellowship with a predictable income, and had decent reserves and inbound invoice payments, so we were able to weather the incident relatively gracefully in financial terms. But I couldn't help but run the counterfactual in my head: what if this had happened when I'd been in a cash-flow slump with low reserves and no invoices due, and no longer gigs on the horizon? Or worse, on the cusp of a major spike-income gig that I might have had to turn down? It might have been enough to knock me out of the game, drain all my reserves, drive me into long-term credit card debt, and force me to look for a paycheck job on an emergency basis.

This is not a theoretical scenario. I've come close to that condition 3–4 times in the last decade, but fortunately never actually had to drop out. But my wife and I still have three elderly living parents between us, plus all the usual risks everybody faces: illness, disability, catastrophic losses, and so forth. And insurance can only play a limited role in managing this risk. Much of the risk mitigation has to come from cash flow management and savings/investment habits. The line between continued survival in the gig economy and crashing out of it is a very thin one, no matter how long you've been in the game. Don't get complacent about either the risks, or why the risks are worth taking on (short answer: freedom).

ANTIFRAGILE GIGWORK

Can small businesses and gig economy careers be *made* antifragile by clever design? There's evidence that there's some room for that. Research on corporate longevity out of Royal Dutch/Shell, which led to an interesting book called *The Living Company* by Arie de Gues, suggests that there are two key factors:

1. One of those factors is an open, experimental culture. Nice. You and I, brave exploratory adventurers of the gig economy, we've got that covered.
2. The other factor, unfortunately, is simply levels of reserve resources. Financial conservatism in short. Yikes.

Unfortunately, I think the second factor is by far more important for smaller businesses, and almost the whole factor for indies. This finding jibes with the observation, in Bill Janeway's book on the startup economy, *Doing Capitalism in the Innovation Economy*, that what gets startups through turbulent times is simply *cash and control*. Cash reserves (raise more funding than you need if you expect a downturn, and hold on to it) and control (keep control of your company/board) constitute startup survival 101.

I think we can reasonably extrapolate such findings to the gig economy, with extreme added prejudice. These ideas apply much more strongly to us, since our incomes are usually based neither on securitizable assets like restaurants, nor on VC-investible activities like startups. We generally do not have access to OPM (Other People's Money) even for things paycheck people take for granted, like home buying. This picture is changing. Now that I've been in the game long enough, I routinely get working capital loan offers from services like Paypal and Stripe (as well as scammy offers via shady phone calls). But it's very limited kind of access to OPM and definitely not cheap capital. More importantly, I don't feel comfortable taking on that kind of OPM debt without a more capital-building type plan to generate a higher return rate than the interest rate. And most of us in the gig economy aren't building up capital assets, only goodwill and reputation. If we were, we'd be startups.

The question is, can we do anything about these operating conditions, or are we doomed to be the canaries in the coal mine of the economy at large, the first to get slaughtered by bad times?

ARE YOU A LINDY INDIE?

Nassim Taleb popularized a good lens on fragility: the Lindy effect. Applied to our problem, the idea is, if a thing has survived for n years, you should expect it to survive for another n years. I've been surviving in the gig economy since March 2011 and if my hustle is Lindy as of 2022, expect me to be in business till March 2033.

The Lindy effect is something of an untrustworthy blackbox model though. You can't just *assume* it holds. You have to open up the box and figure out if, how, and why. Then, perhaps, you can pose *Lindy* as a design challenge to solve for. If you accept the openness+reserves model I referenced and approximate survivability as just a function of reserves, Lindyness is really just a kind of 1:1 ratio between expenses run rate and reserves accumulation run rate. A very simplistic model looks something like the illustration on the following page.

The reserves might be in many forms: liquid cash and cash-equivalents. Assets like home equity you could use for securitized debt. Accounts receivable. Relatively low-maintenance income streams like ebook sales that won't turn off overnight if you stop maintaining them.

But whatever form they take, being a Lindy Indie really just boils down to building up reserves. Far more reserves than paycheck economy types build, because we in the gig economy typically lack the risk-underwriting benefits of being tethered to a larger, less fragile entity.

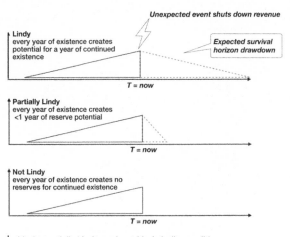

| Lindy, partially Lindy, and not-Lindy indie conditions

This goes beyond just structural effects of employment itself, to things like having a strong community of friends and colleagues who might pitch in and help you when you're in trouble. For most working adults, a significant fraction of their *social* capital is *also* tied to being in a job. Indies have to make do with a much smaller social safety net of close friends and family they can call on.

So where does that leave us? If we want to be Lindy Indies, we kinda have to design Lindyness into our businesses ourselves. The brute force answer is to simply cut down expenses till they are half the after-tax income, saving the other half in conservative reserve form (cash).

This is a shitty answer and basically impossible for most of us. Are there better answers? We are going to find out in the next few decades.

9

THE GIGWORK HIERARCHY OF NEEDS

A MODEL OF GIGWORK

IT IS time for me to do a proper guided tour of the ground we've covered so far so you can see and navigate the bigger picture taking shape, and get a sense of my cunning plan to catalyze a Brave New Age of Gigwork.

The key to both is this Maslow-esque hierarchy of needs diagram (next page).

TOWARDS A FULL-STACK CONVERSATION

The current larger conversation about the gig economy is almost entirely—to the tune of 90%—bogged down in the two bottom layers of the pyramid in the diagram, narrowly concerned with questions of lead-conversion rates and financial survival over a <2 year strategy horizon. By contrast, the corresponding conversations about regular careers, or startup entrepreneurship, are much more mature and full-stack, covering the entire equivalent pyramids, and lifespan-length horizons.

When I started out in 2011, there was little to no useful advice out there on how to actually go about crafting a satisfying and meaningful life out of internet-enabled gigwork. Much of what I read amounted to religious ranting about the moral superiority of free agency, cargo-cult "systems," uncritical dogmas about the superiority of "value-added" consulting, ethically dubious arbitrage games, and most worryingly, widespread predatory contempt for clients (paradoxically alloyed with whining victimhood).

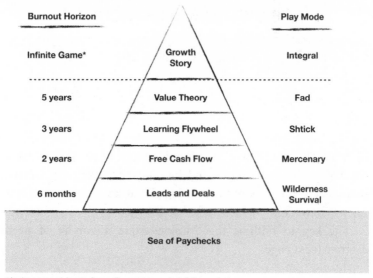

* In the sense of James Carse. Does not mean indefinite survival.

Gigwork Hierarchy of Needs

And of course, lots of exhortations to aggressively chase leads, spray-and-pray pitches at potential clients, and generally be an obnoxious, glad-handing hustler 24x7. The gig economy is not immune to hustleporn.

Much of what I read was actually lazy ports of how-to wisdom from two sources: entrepreneurship and sales. Almost all of it was useless because indie consulting and gigwork are *not* like either of those activities. The superficial base-layer similarities—necessary reliance on a conversion funnel, and precarious cash flow—leads people to ignore deeper and more consequential differences.

I decided very early on—like a couple of months in—that if success and survival in the gig economy meant exhausting zombie hustling and soulless grinding, I didn't want it. So I decided to figure out my own playbook. I've now been running that playbook for over a decade, with dozens of clients, so I think I can say with some confidence that the Art of Gig playbook I'm laying out here has been validated at least at an $n=1$ level.

My goal with this book is to try and level up the conversation around gigwork into a full-stack conversation, where people like you and me are talking about all levels, rather than just the bottom levels. So here is a tour of the territory surveyed so far, sorted by level.

LEADS AND DEALS

The newbie leads-and-deals level of indie consulting is, in my opinion, best tackled by diving right into the deep end, with just a vague idea of what you're going to do, and a few months worth of savings to live off while you figure it out. What you're solving for at this level is simply leads and (closed) deals, and bringing in the money by any means necessary.

But it's a mistake to try and work that problem directly, by playing it like a formulaic numbers game the way sales people sometimes do. It may work in the short term, but it's a recipe for very quick burnout. As with any kind of gambling, be wary of people selling you "systems" that are "guaranteed" to deliver a certain return rate in conversions and closed deals.

No "system" to enter indie consulting survives first contact with a *No!* from a potential client, or the first bout of cash-flow panic. So it's best to just dive right in. Just focus on making money any way you can, and acquiring your own idiosyncratic understanding of how the game is played. You can worry about theorizing your model later.

FREE CASH FLOW

If you get stuck in the leads-and-deals level, you probably won't last longer than six months. Even if your funnel is converting well, and generating enough income to live on. Unless you leave that base layer within about six months, you will experience burnout due to the sheer joylessness of the grind at that level of the game. To get to the next level you need to focus on *free cash flow*.

As an indie consultant, you are primarily an investor in yourself. The best principle for making this investment is the venture-capital principle of *cash and control*. The more you have a strong, liquid cash position, and control over your life, the easier it becomes to be strategic and rational about pricing your services right and saying *yes* or *no* to gigs based on considerations *other* than rent-panic levels.

At this level, you're basically learning to run your indie consulting life as a business, and acquire and refine basic instincts around pricing, supply and demand for your services, and negotiations, *all driven by an understanding of your own needs, lifestyle costs, and operating margins.*

LEARNING FLYWHEEL

If you get stuck at the free-cash flow level, and never get beyond solving for maximum money with minimum time investment, and maximal cash and control (this is the basic flaw of the 4-hour-workweek approach) you will burn out in about two years. To last longer, you have to discover who you are, by doubling down on things you like to learn, *while working on gigs.*

It's a bad mistake to separate your learning interests from your working interests. That's a recipe for eventually hating your work, thinking of it as just a way to pay the bills and fund your fun, and an activity that you'd rather make passive and get yourself out of. It rarely works.

In other words, once you have a robust dealflow going and enough cash and control to actually be able to run your indie consulting life as a sustainable business in non-panic mode, you can start saying *yes* and *no* more thoughtfully to opportunities and start spinning up a unique learning flywheel within your gigwork.

At the learning flywheel level, you should strive to say *yes* to gigs where you'll learn more of what you want to learn, and *no* to gigs where you won't. It's as simple as that.

And it's the opposite of passive income. This is as active as income gets. You're not looking for shortcuts. You're looking to make the long way the fun way.

Why? Because at this point, you are solving the problem of figuring out who you are. This is effectively indistinguishable from what you're learning the fastest, which in turn is almost entirely a function of what behaviors you are *repeating most frequently* and *enjoying* in your gigs. In other words, *the iteration rate of mindful deliberate practice.*

Finding and staying in the maximal iteration/learning rate zone of what you enjoy is a pretty subtle challenge. It took me nearly three years to figure out that it was "conversational sparring" for me. You have to scope your gigs right, have lots of the right kinds of conversations, and be very productive in the right kind of deliverable medium.

VALUE THEORY

Believe it or not—and this is heresy to doerists—a life of pure learning and new personal records is *not* satisfying. If you get stuck at the learning level, you will burn out in about three years. To survive longer, you have to explore how you create value for others.

Once you have a sense of confidence in who you are, through success in your learning efforts and a stably spinning flywheel, you can start to expand your horizons. You can look at your role in the world of work critically and ask *what am I doing here?* in a relatively disinterested way, without being insecurely attached to your hard-won skills.

When you've bootstrapped this level of mindful ongoing inter-rogation of your working life, you will be able to more readily see the world from the point of view of your clients, critically interro-gate your own evolving identity, and become aware of your blindspots, rationalizations, and limiting self-perceptions.

It is necessary to have established this ongoing interrogative process as a set of habits *before* you can meaningfully ask the ques-tion, *how do I actually create or add value?* If you ask it too early, you will only find ritualistic, self-serving answers.

GROWTH STORY

If you get stuck at the value level, you will last perhaps five years before you burn out due to either extreme idealism or extreme cynicism. Unfortunately, a clear-eyed questioning of whether you're adding value will often yield the answer, *no.* And you can get sucked in from there into perennial agonizing and fine-tuning of your work, in an attempt to find a Grand Unified Theory of Guar-anteed Value Addition.

This is a utopian trap. You're actually doing far better than average if you can claim that you are adding value in one out of two gigs. A more typical rate I suspect is one in five (below that, you'll likely feel like you're participating in a bullshit-work economy).

The corresponding dystopian trap is coming to believe that nothing can ever get better, and slowly succumbing to the tempta-tions of fraud, bad faith, and corruption.

The growth story level is about making your peace with the best effectiveness of impact you are able to generate, without falling victim to either utopian idealism or dystopian cynicism. One of the reasons many indie consultants fail to do this, and get trapped at the value theory level is that they fail to distinguish learning (one level below) from growth (one level above). They think the value-theory level is the top of the pyramid.

Learning is a matter of disciplined curiosity, conscious cultivation of knowledge and skills, and strategic choice of gigs. You can learn without really growing, and many people do exactly that. That's how you get trapped in shticks.

You can also learn within a fixed theory of value addition and grow complacent within a fixed sense of your own worth. That's how you become part of a faddish trend. A fad is basically an uncritical, fixed, widely shared value theory that only dies when it starts to fail miserably, triggering utopian or dystopian yearnings and behaviors.

Growth is the result of *integrating your experiences, figuring out what they mean, healing any scars, and evolving beyond them.* This means reflecting on what happens to you and to the world around you, as a result of you doing what you do, *and extracting the right lessons.* How do you know when the lessons are the right ones? When they point the way to continuing the game in the most interesting way possible, instead of adding more details to the map of whatever value-addition rut you are in.

This is a storytelling task. You have to repeatedly tell both your own story, and the story of your environment, at all scales, and maintain a constant, live sense of how you're part of a bigger story.

10

THE PRICE OF FREEDOM
THE FUNDAMENTAL CHOICES AND
CONSEQUENCES OF GIGWORK

GIGWORK IS A NEGATIVELY DEFINED LIFESTYLE—IT is a lifestyle where the constraints of paycheck employment do not apply. Nor do the burdens of leadership responsibilities. We have the freedom to make choices people in traditional careers cannot. This freedom comes with a price tag, however. Let's look at the consequences of our choices.

Consider this pick-2-of-3 triangle, with vertices labeled *autonomy of goals, integrity of methods,* and *standard of living.* For the moment, trust me that you can't have all three. Think about what you're most willing to give up. Identify your current choice.

| Phase 1: You make choices

CONSEQUENCES

Done? You didn't peek ahead?

Okay. *Consequences.* Look at the side defined by your two choices (opposite the vertex you sacrificed) on the next version of this diagram below. Those are the *consequences* you can expect, within about a year or so.

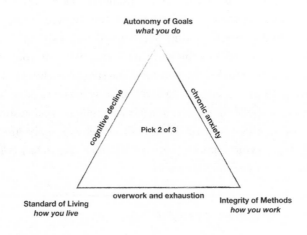

| Phase 2: There are consequences!

When you give up *integrity of methods* (in terms of skilled discipline and/or ethics) you break the feedback loop of mindful practice and growth that keeps your cognitive abilities and procedural-ethical judgments strong and growing. So you experience cognitive decline.

When you give up *standard of living*, you experience chronic anxiety, but this is of a subtle variety. The thing is, the anxiety is not caused by decline in standard of living itself, but social factors. You cannot keep up the class lifestyle expected of someone doing the things you are doing. And family and friends are often the biggest sources of this anxiety because you care about them and they care about you. This dissonance between how you work and how you must live to conform to the expectations of your milieu creates chronic anxiety and increasing financial worry.

When you give up *autonomy of goals* (i.e., cede agency over deciding what's worth doing/caring about and why) you can generally expect to get a lot more work. There is always a lot of demand for people who will do what they're told within a sharply bounded scope, no questions asked. And you will tend to take the work, because you will start to measure your life by the numbers that get driven up by sheer quantity of work—dollars, fawning testimonials, awards. And you will find yourself getting overworked and exhausted. Again there's a subtlety. It's not the work itself that exhausts you, but the fact that you have to do it to a professional standard while studiously not caring (or pretending not to care) about why you're doing it, and for whom. Suspending the need for meaningfulness is exhausting!

But wait, there's more! We're not done! Not only are there *consequences* to your choices, there are *natural compensatory behaviors* that kick in, almost unconsciously.

NATURAL PATTERNS OF COMPENSATION

You may not realize what you're getting yourself into with your sacrifices until much later, but your subconscious tends to catch on and start doing its thing. Look at the next phrase on your side of the triangle to predict what it will do (next page).

You will compensate for *cognitive decline* by seeking out skilled hobbies and interests and narrow paths of personal accomplishment with feedback loops of strengthening high-integrity behaviors. This temporarily relieves the sense of decline, like scratching an itch, and restores confidence, without addressing the root cause.

You will compensate for *chronic social anxiety* by investing increasing energy into premium mediocrity[1] (looking more successful than you actually are). Again, this temporarily relieves the social pressure and anxiety symptoms without addressing the root cause. You will compensate for *overwork and exhaustion* with hedonistic excess. The finest wines! The finest clothes! The best business cards! Giving up on the search for meaning displaces those instincts to peripheral consumption tastes and pleasure orientation. Again, this only temporarily relieves the growing lack of meaning and sense of a void at the core of your work, without addressing the root cause.

We're still not done! When you give in to natural, subconscious compensatory impulses for too long, leaving root causes unaddressed, you will naturally get to a point where that spells a particular ugly end for you.

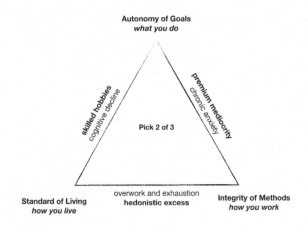

| Phase 3: Natural pattern of compensation

ENDGAMES

Here's how your story ends down each of the three paths, if you don't do something to alter course (diagram next page). If you neglect *integrity of methods* for long enough, you will end up irrelevant and ridiculed as a faddish joke from another era and eventually forgotten. If you neglect *standard of living* for long enough, you

will descend into shameful poverty as you eventually fail to keep up
even premium mediocre appearances.

If you neglect *autonomy of goals* for long enough, your fate is
descent into corruption and moral decay, as you gradually lose
your moral compass and make increasingly terrible decisions. Each
questionable decision will make the next one easier.

So that's what's in store for you down each of the pick-two-of-
three paths. Grim, huh? Yes, but you can fix it, in one of three ways.

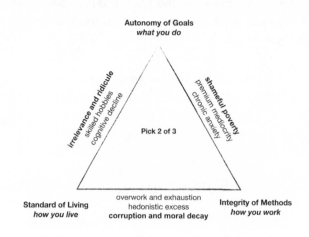

| Phase 4: If left unchecked, *terminal decline*

THE FIX!

First, you can always increase your level of ambition, and grow
beyond gigwork. Of course, you'll end up with different tradeoffs
and constraints to navigate, but maybe that's the challenge you
want next. Second, you can always try to go back to the world of
traditional jobs if you can and accept the constraints there. A good
job will usually offer all three. You know the price-tag that comes
with that, otherwise you wouldn't be reading this book. But sometimes that price tag can become acceptable when life circumstances
change.

But third: if you want to stay in the gig economy, you can hack the triangle! Yes, you have to pick two of three, *but you don't have to make the same choices in all situations and at all times.* You can rotate through them in various creative ways! This creates a much more unstable lifestyle, but it allows you to address the root causes of the pathologies that lie in wait down each pure path. It's like keeping a set of spinning plates spinning by darting among them. There are three basic ways to do this.[2]

Gig-division multiplexing (GDM): Have multiple parallel gigs going, where you pick a different 2/3 in each. This may take a while to spin up since in the early days you may be in wing-and-prayer serial-monogamy gig mode.

Time-division multiplexing (TDM): Depending on circumstances and what constraints are tight or loose at any given time, pick a different 2/3. If you are flush from neglecting goal autonomy last quarter, ease off on the money-making and take a meaningful lower-priced or pro-bono gig (I recommend lower-priced/smaller over pro-bono; pro-bono work comes with its own baggage that needs careful handling).

Activity-division multiplexing (ADM): Every gig is multiple strands of interwoven activity. You don't have to make the same 2/3 choices in all strands. For example, you can compromise on integrity of methods on presentation and packaging while sticking rigorously to your methods in the backend analysis and thinking work for example. There will nearly always be ways to make such factorizations. So there you go. Make your choices. Accept the consequences in the short term, but resist them in the long term. Make new choices when and where you can, in order to avoid degenerating.

That's the price of freedom: you have to stay mindful of the consequences of your choices, and change them as necessary, across the duration and scope of your career, at varying resolutions. Freedom is for what Samo Burja calls *live players.*[3] If you act dead, you will eventually die for real in an unpleasant way.

1. www.ribbonfarm.com/2017/08/17/the-premium-mediocre-life-of-maya-millennial/
2. These are roughly analogous to FDMA, TDMA, and CDMA multiplexing strategies in communications engineering.
3. medium.com/@samo.burja/live-versus-dead-players-2b24f6e9eae2

11

LESSONS FROM THE BIG THREE
WHAT CAN INDIE CONSULTANTS LEARN FROM MCKINSEY, BAIN, AND BCG?

IN LAST CHAPTER I WROTE:

When you give up integrity of methods (in terms of skilled discipline and/or ethics) you break the feedback loop of mindful practice and growth that keeps your cognitive abilities and procedural-ethical judgments strong and growing. So you experience cognitive decline.

I want to revisit this point a bit, in light of the growing bad press and hostile scrutiny the Big Three consulting firms—McKinsey, Bain, and BCG—have been subject to in recent ears. The various "revelations" fueling the reputational assault on the Big Three weren't really news, in the sense of not being even remotely surprising to anyone who knows how the consulting industry works. What was actually news is that this counted as news for the broader public.

The interesting question for me is: what exactly does the general public *think* the Big Three firms do? That they sometimes work in sketchy ways, and are not too picky about who they work for, is not exactly a secret. It is unclear what illusions, held by whom, are being shattered.

The question is important for us in the indie consulting world. In many ways The Big Three are bellwethers for perceptions of consulting in general, including the indie variety. So the fates of the two sectors are coupled, and shifts in sectoral perceptions matter to us. The big difference is that the kinds of incentives and pressures firms like McKinsey navigate as companies, you and I navigate as individuals (albeit at a much smaller scale). This means the mindfulness feedback loop I refer to above is much easier for us to maintain in a healthy state. It is also much harder for us to ignore problems with the feedback loop.

For big consulting firms, much of the responsibility for big decisions rests with senior partners, rather than with the rank-and-file who do much of the grinding on engagements, so the feedback loop is vulnerable to being broken.

As independent consultants, you and I cannot blame senior partners for poor judgment, or rank-and-file grinders for failures in execution. We are responsible for both judgment and execution. If the feedback loop breaks, it's our own fault. If we are held accountable for behaviors of clients we are complicit in, our options for deflecting the blame are limited.

KNIVES OUT

The last decade has been a decade of bad optics and brand tarnishing for McKinsey and its peers. It started in 2012 with the conviction of then-CEO of McKinsey, Rajat Gupta, for insider trading, and an unflattering spotlight on Bain thanks to the presidential bid of Mitt Romney. It was followed more recently by a harsh media spotlight on McKinsey for its work with Saudi Arabia and the Trump regime. The big-firm consulting sector today no longer enjoys the high regard it did in the aughts, though students in MBA programs appear not to have caught on yet.

The reaction to the most recent round of bad press was swift and harsh. Matt Stoller published a scathing indictment.[1] Louis Hyman, a historian of capitalism at the Cornell School of Industrial and Labor Relations posted a Twitter thread[2] blaming McKinsey (somewhat unfairly) for inventing the modern, precarious gig economy. Others gleefully jumped in with whatever pent-up hostilities towards the sector they had been harboring. The knives came out in earnest.

None of the revelations was news of course, which is why many of us were puzzled. Nobody ever pretended the Big Three consulting firms were *not* what these sensational "revelations" were showing them unambiguously to be. What had changed was the public mood in relation to what Walter Kiechel called the literary-industrial complex, which includes (besides prestigious consulting firms) elite universities, research centers like the MIT Media Lab, business book publishing, and events like TED and Davos.

The mood shifted from tolerant and indulgent to harsh and unforgiving. Recent years have not been a good time to be affiliated with the literary-industrial complex, if you care about public perceptions.

In 1999, the Mike Judge comedy *Office Space* portrayed consultants as unprincipled sociopaths, but still people to be regarded more sympathetically than the clueless fat-cat executives and managers they supported. People who genuinely relished the intellectual challenge of whipping a struggling company back into shape, and who did meaningful, if not always pleasant, things towards that end. Despite all the jokes, Big Consulting has generally *not* been regarded as bullshit work over its short history. For better or worse, it has been too consequential and self-aware to dismiss with that particular criticism.

What changed? Why are consulting firms suddenly being held accountable, in the court of public opinion, for the decisions of their clients? Why has the get-out-of-jail-free card stopped working?

Up until the Great Recession, the perception of the Big-Three large-scale consulting industry was largely positive, as cunning rascals you had to grudgingly admire. They were seen as bagmen doing the dirty work bankers and CEOs made necessary. Deliverers of harsh messages. And at their best, pragmatic mercenary foils mitigating missionary tendencies towards ideological excess. They were seen as aware of, and complicit in, high-level governance in all parts of the institutional landscape, but ultimately not primarily responsible for moral matters.

These perceptions matter to us in the indie consulting world because, like I said, they trickle down to shape how we are perceived as well, which for the most part we've welcomed as a positive. In some cases, I've made direct reference to them in positioning what I do, as in "I do the same sort of stuff McKinsey does, just on my own, and at a lower price." It's not actually a very accurate self-characterization, but it is a good-enough starter perception, while I establish my actual modes of delivering value.

But these perceptions have changed, and with them, the consequences of positioning yourself relative to the Big Three. The cost of co-marketing convenience has changed.

Now, increasingly, the big consulting firms are seen as directly responsible for the moral failures of client organizations. Even perhaps *more* responsible than client leaders. They are seen as predatory organizations that exploit the general stupidity and incompetence in prey firms to capture them for profit, by making themselves indispensable to running them, but without any accountability for running them *well*. It's a cousin of regulatory capture.

And there is some justification there that favors the consulting firms. Many large organizations are so dysfunctional, they effectively *have* to be run by the big-firm consultants who service them. They are too brain-dead to run themselves unassisted (a condition the big consulting firms had a hand in creating). A good part of the consulting market is a corporate assisted-living facility for geriatric companies.

But that justification begs the question to some extent. If the organizations are so brain-dead they need to be on consulting-firm life support to function, it is a little disingenuous to claim that ethics decisions on matters of mission and values are entirely the client's problem. A generalized zombie is obviously also specifically a moral zombie, incompetent to stand trial.

Who is asking whether the zombie clients should exist at all? Why should such relationships be viewed as anything other than pure scavenging or parasitism in the guise of guardianship? Turns out, there's actually an interesting answer here.

GRINDER SELECTION EFFECTS

I've been largely sympathetic to McKinsey and its peers through most of my adult working life. Many of my classmates and friends have spent time with one of them. I interviewed with McKinsey in 2003 while finishing up my Ph.D. and got rejected in the second round. I didn't mind though. It was so obvious that I did not fit the grinder profile they were recruiting for, it made me respect rather than resent their selection process.

That's the most important thing you have to understand about the Big-Three consulting world: *it selects for intelligent, high-energy grinders, not snowflake philosophers driven by foundational curiosities.* People who set out early in life to win the game as it is presented to them, rather than question, subvert, or change it. Which is not *ipso facto* a bad thing. If the game presented to such people is a good one, they will play it well, and a good time will be had by all. The world runs on grinders. When it runs at all.

What the critics miss in calling out the unsurprising fact that inexperienced college grads are rented out at a high markup (not in itself problematic as far as I am concerned) is just how hard and effectively these people are willing to work, compared to the complacent and comfortable managers at the organizations they serve. I'd be dead in a month if I tried to work at the pace I've seen young Big-Three consultants work. 100-hour weeks are not uncommon. The lifestyle of constant, stressful travel, and living out of hotels, takes a toll too. Whatever their sins, taking it easy isn't one of them. And whatever my virtues, working that hard isn't one of them.

I was clearly not cut out for their approach. When I struck out on my own, that early rejection helped me define the kind of consulting I could actually be good at, and could sustainably do at the level of effort I am capable of putting out (which is about 0.1G, where 1G=1 Grinder). I could position myself in a differentiated way around conversational sparring, and avoid anything that looked like a Big Three 100-hour grind. I could benefit from the perceptions of the consulting industry, but not be bound, limited, or defined by them.

That grinder selection effect that dominates the Big-Three world is at once its greatest strength and greatest weakness. As a strength: there are few forces in the world comparable to the raw mid-grade aggregated intellectual horsepower that can be unleashed on organizational problems by the likes of McKinsey, Bain, and BCG. And it's easy to underestimate it because what an individual junior associate does can seem like unimpressive grinding. But a dozen such people grinding in the right places can move mountains. Or Fortune 100 companies.

As Matt Stoller noted in his criticism, the problems these firms solve are not exactly difficult, and the advice they end up offering is not exactly genius-grade. But the point is, it *does* require fairly intelligent grinding at scale to generate that advice, with the right numbers and specific details attached.

Finding cost-cutting opportunities in a large corporation is rarely about elegant strategic insight and 2x2s. It is usually an exercise in sending a small army of Excel-armed young associates into every corner of the company, documenting costs, and figuring out where to make cuts by crunching the numbers. And that's not an activity that trains you much in asking the hard questions about why you're trying to make cuts in the first place, or why the organization exists in the world, and whether perhaps it should not. Grinding mainly teaches you to grind in more efficient ways.

To be clear, this is work that large companies and organizations are generally *not* actually capable of doing for themselves. They are too compromised by infighting and self-serving delusions and blindspots. What the big consulting armies are selling is not genius brainpower, stellar imagination, reserves of courage, philosophical insight, or even skilled labor time. They are selling the distance that enables them to look in places internal eyes cannot look, and turns impossible problems into manageable grinds.

At *scale*. They are the organizational equivalent of expensive medical imaging equipment. To complain that inexperienced young graduates are being paid big bucks to "run the playbook" is like complaining that medical technicians rather than doctors are operating medical imaging equipment. The value lies in the machine, or in this case, the scalable procedural machine defined by the playbook, not the operators running it.

But as a weakness: selection for grinders is a selection of people with little philosophical interest in matters of principle, impatience with doctrinal thinking, disdain for reflection, and a bias towards hard-driving action. People with those devalued cognitive strengths within these firms (if they get into these firms in the first place) tend to get sidelined into functional expertise areas where they might write modest whitepapers and books that don't rock the boat, provide occasional injections of spot expertise on special topics, and do thought-leadership work rather than frontline consulting work.

Those miscast on the grinder frontlines, or with too much maladaptive talent for the devalued kinds of thinking, tend to burn out early and drop out. They typically don't last long enough to make partner or execute a smart sideways shift into a VP role on the client side. So there is a strong adverse selection process at work here. At the tops of these firms, there is not just a disciplined tendency to stay away from doctrinal matters, *but a systematic functional weakness in the capacity to think about them in the first place.*

The problem with firms like McKinsey isn't that they aid and abet organizations pursuing unaccountable missions that the broader public might find problematic. The problem is that grinders aren't philosophers. Which is not to valorize or demonize either. Just an observation that the two are not the same thing, which is a problem if you believe, as I do, that both have a role to play, and either pretends to be both.

STRATEGY SANS ETHICS

The self-labels the Big-Three firms use are interesting and revealing. All bill themselves "strategy" firms, and "strategy" is a coveted aspirational label for second-tier IT and marketing consulting firms eyeing their market from a middle-layer position. The cachet of "strategy" also continues to attract aggressively competitive and ambitious graduates of elite universities determined to grind their way to the top of elite institutional society, and be counted among the movers and shakers of the world at Davos some day, fluidly navigating the top echelons of global power.

But what does "strategy" mean for these firms? Historically, for McKinsey it has meant being present in boardrooms and C-suites, and participating in decisions at that level, but not getting involved in execution. For Bain it has meant specializing in shareholder-value hacking. For BCG it has meant brainiac "insights" for framing big moves.

Or as I like to think of it, Gryffindor, Slytherin, and Ravenclaw.[3]

What is missing across the board in this sector is a sense of *strategy* that includes genuine, and deeply considered, doctrinal, ethical, or philosophical elements (which to me are indispensable components) driven by real curiosity on those fronts. For the Big

Three, those are regarded as the client's concerns, and decoupled from strategic considerations proper. They are also generally regarded as matters of cosmetics and optics, rather than concerns integral to business models, worth taking seriously.

And of course, in practice, 90% of top executives don't want to be holding the ethics and philosophy balls either, and tend to quietly drop them when nobody is looking.

One side effect of this abdication of ethics responsibilities by both C-suite leaders and their prestige-firm consultants is that those responsibilities end up devolved to HR and legal departments, whence they are further farmed out to a boutique gig-economy cottage industry of what I think of as *ethics theaters*. This is people who gleefully go around creating workshops, training regimens, compliance bureaucracies, and exhausting rules regimes around every aspect of individual and corporate behavior. All mostly aimed at creating plausible deniability on some ethics front, and cushy jobs for internal ethics czars. The situation resembles medieval milieus, where commercial life was heavily governed by a host of arbitrary sumptuary laws and enforced performative behaviors, imposed by various unaccountable moral authority figures.

Any activity that attracts a derisive -*washing* suffix, such as "greenwashing," is almost certainly an example of such an ethics theater. The DEI and ESG theaters are the latest examples of such boutique sectors, where you are more likely to find grifters or power-tripping political opportunists than people sincerely engaging with the actual ethics issues supposedly in question.

So the cost of abdicating responsibility for the moral dimension at the top is a bloated ethics-grifter bureaucracy in the middle, which has the potential to eventually grow into a cancer that threatens the organization's life without particularly elevating its ethics game.

The party line in the consulting world is: the client sets broad objectives based on their CEO values, corporate values, missions, and so forth, and we help figure out how to operationalize it in strategy, by doing the detailed research, creating the justifications necessary, and recommending effective paths.

It is something of a lawyerly stance: the client is something like a defendant in a court of law and it's the consultant's job to build the most effective case allowing them to do what they want to do. Passing judgment and doling out punishments and rewards is for juries and judges. For the private sector, that means the court of public and market opinion. For government agencies and politicians, it means the voting public. In any case, it's not the consultant's job.

This is a convenient position to take if your goal is to accept the widest range of moneyed clients possible. Work for a dictatorship and a democracy at the same time? No problem, we'll do both and let the political philosophers work out the meanings. You want to solve for sustainability, profitability, or lowering the cost of incarceration of prisoners or illegal immigrants? No problem, we'll make you a spreadsheet model for any and all of it, and dig up the numbers necessary to populate it.

It is tempting to conclude that this is an ethically malicious position to adopt out of convenience, and an aspect of the moral hazards of the principal-agent relationship inherent in consulting. Why take responsibility for stuff you don't have to? There's clearly no upside.

The real explanation is more sobering: the adverse-selection mechanism by which these firms staff themselves with grinders ensures that the majority of people working in them are genuinely not even *capable* of processing such questions meaningfully.

It's a cousin of Hanlon's razor: never attribute to malice what can be adequately explained by unexamined philosophical commitments. In this case, we're talking about an adversely selected disinterest in philosophical foundations on the consulting side, and a deliberate abdication of moral responsibilities (accompanied by devolution of the responsibilities to middle-management staff functions) by client leadership. Either way, the outcome is that the judgment of the court of public opinion, and eventually, the market, is harsh. And when times turn dark, the knives come out.

My own judgment is perhaps less harsh, mostly because I don't expect anything better from the big consulting industry, and don't share the illusions that many apparently have (or are conveniently pretending to have) about the sector. They are what they are, and they do what they do.

I don't have any bright ideas for how the Big consulting companies can change, or whether they even should attempt to do so, since we're talking about features rather than bugs in their core DNA. But then, I'm not entirely sure the sector needs to exist at all.

My null hypothesis is that organizations that are zombified enough that they cannot run themselves without Big Consulting support perhaps shouldn't continue to exist, and deserve to be disrupted and displaced by organizations that can do the necessary thinking on their own (with some modest help from us indie consultants of course). And if the market left over when you eliminate the zombie-life-extension segment isn't big enough to sustain Big Consulting, perhaps Big Consulting needs to shrink.

To me, ultimately, ethics in consulting is simple: it's a matter of saying no to things. Which usually means lowering some topline or bottomline expectations, and being content with less. Ethics are a form of self-imposed taxation. Perhaps you can creatively make up for these tax losses with growth elsewhere, but you can't magically transform the tax-like nature of the beast. You just have to decide that you believe in the things the taxes pay for, and hope that paying those taxes benefits you in unknown ways in the future. If you knew the actual incentives and payoffs for behaving in ethical ways, it would be part of strategy, not ethics.

That's a decision that's easy to make as an indie consultant, but quite hard when you're a huge company staffed by an army of grinders all expecting to climb to the top, and led by people who have been grinding so hard, for so long, they can't see past grinding as an end in itself to existential questions about themselves or their clients. They live in a world of TINA assumptions—*There is No Alternative*. A world of elites that has always been run a certain way, around a set of sacrosanct institutional compromises. A way in which they have an indispensable and well-paid role to play. A role that takes hard work to fill. A role they cannot imagine being fulfilled any other way. If you could imagine a different way, you wouldn't be working in that world.

We'll see if they're right in the next few decades.

LESSONS FOR INDIES

To return to my opening self-quote, the mindfulness feedback loop for staying ethically grounded is much easier for us indies to maintain than for big firms, but it's not trivial.

The big lesson for independent consultants is that strategy decisions are always also moral decisions. Every client you accept, every task you accept, has both strategic *and* moral implications for you and the client. And even if you both operate in strictly legal ways, and perfectly within the bounds of the contracts that govern your relationships, you're *still* going to be held morally accountable for the work you chose to do.

And as I pointed out in the opening, as an independent, you will never have the luxury of blaming someone else for your choices, the way people in big firms do. The only excuses that will ever be available to you as an indie consultant, for anything you choose to do, are "I needed the money" and "it was perfectly legal and aboveboard." Neither excuse has a history of flying well in the face of hostile public scrutiny.

So doing the right thing is, in the long term, the easiest thing if you're in the indie consulting world, and want to be able to withstand hostile scrutiny with nothing to apologize for or be ashamed about. You don't have enough maneuvering room to do anything else. Big firms get themselves into trouble largely because they have the maneuvering room to do so, not because they are morally worse than independent consultants.

This is not abstract theory for me. I've said no to potential clients when I've been in need of money. I've said no to doing specific tasks long-term clients have asked of me. But I'm also no saint. After all, my reputation is based primarily on writings recommending slightly evil sociopathic behaviors. But I'm happy to own that. The point is, whatever you do, and wherever on the spectrum from absolute saint to absolute sinner you choose to land, you can actually choose to own it in a way big companies generally cannot. So make your choices. Carefully.

---

1. mattstoller.substack.com/p/why-taxpayers-pay-mckinsey-3m-a-year
2. twitter.com/louishyman/status/1202105533559443457
3. Hufflepuffs are the strategy-wannabe second-tier IT and marketing firms.

12

TEN DIMENSIONS OF GIGWORK

ARE YOU A CONSULTANT, CONTRACTOR, OR PLATFORMER? 10 WAYS TO TELL

SO FAR, I've been rather sloppy in talking about distinctions among three kinds of gig economy workers: indie consultants, indie contractors, and under-the-API gigworkers, who I'm now relabeling as *platformers* (people who find work via platforms like Uber or Upwork, and to whom I can't with a straight face attach the adjective *indie*). Let's clean up our definitions of these three important categories and their structural relationships to each other. First, here is the basic structure, with a diagram on the next page:

- You're an *indie consultant* if you don't have to deal with gatekeeper organizations, such as purchasing or HR. You may still need to do paperwork with them, but they have little control over whether or not to hire you because sufficiently senior managers or executives are making that call. If hiring freezes/cost control measures are in place, they are senior enough to authorize exceptions, or are irreplaceable enough to get such exceptions made on their behalf via their chain of command (often this is mission-critical technical people).

- You're a *contractor* if a purchasing or HR department has significant power to say *no*, based on a variety of considerations, and the client principal can't override that decision.
- You're an *under-the-API platformer* if you get work mostly on autopilot from a demand-aggregator platform, with little to no human gatekeeping. You might get some procedural human attention while signing up, and during exceptional situations, but that's it.

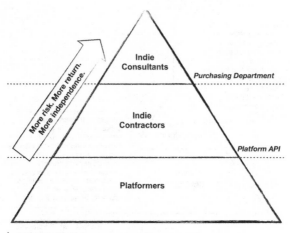

| Three kinds of gig economy workers

How are these three layers different? The overall difference is that you take on more risk for more return in the higher layers, and gain more independence if you succeed. Much of the changing risk/return profile comes from having to sell yourself to generate your own demand. The increased independence manifests as increasing control over contract terms. This basic difference drives all the other differences.

On the next page are ten important dimensions of the differences, illustrated. I've tried to be pretty black-and-white for clarity, but of course, there are blurred edges in all ten dimensions. The ten dimensions (detailed for the three layers above) are: competition mode, social perception, contracting structure, rate-setting, haggling/bidding dynamics, demand structure, selling model, positioning, generic strategy type, and branding.

For most of you, the ambiguity in who you are is likely to be between contracting and consulting. The easiest way to tell the two apart is *whether or not you haggle*, discussed later in *When is a Gig an Engagement?* Important point: as I note there, contractors can often make more money per hour than comparable consultants. Haggling does *not* mean being paid less.

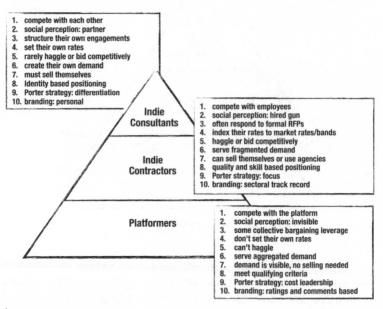

| Ten dimensions of gigwork

But platformers generally *are* paid less (far less) than either contractors or consultants, because they're generally participating in a relatively lower skill sector. Uber-for-X generally involves low-$/hour kinds of X. The simplest way to understand the logic of these distinctions is via Michael Porter's famous generic strategies model[1]:

- indie consultants use a strategy of differentiation
- indie contractors use a strategy of focus
- platformers use a strategy of low-cost leadership

These things are hard to mix effectively, which is why hybrid strategies are dangerous unless you're absolutely forced into them. They require incompatible operating practices and models, so if you hybridize, you'll often find yourself making zero-sum trade-offs. Moves that strengthen you as a contractor will weaken you as a consultant and vice-versa. This is also why upward mobility is rare in the gig economy. You're likely to stay at the level you're at, unless you pull a high-effort stunt to move up.[2]

I imagine very few of you are in the platformer layer, or if you are, it's a temporary way to backstop cash-flow shortfalls while you get the game going at either the contracting or consulting levels. But the reason I pay a lot of attention to the platform layer is that it is the strongest manifestation of "software eating the world" in the gig economy. The biggest trends in the gig economy are unfolding at the platform layer.

So you need to be paying attention to it and open to participating in it if it opens up the right possibilities for you.

---

1. en.wikipedia.org/wiki/Porter%27s_generic_strategies
2. For the contractor to consultant move, a good stunt is to write a book.

13

TOWARDS GIGWORK AS A FOLKWAY

INVENTING THE FUTURE OF THE GIG ECONOMY

LATELY, I have started thinking of the gig economy as a full-fledged *folkway*, which historian David Hackett Fischer defined as:

> the normative structure of values, customs and meanings that exist in any culture. This complex is not many things but one thing, with many interlocking parts. . . . Folkways do not rise from the unconscious in even a symbolic sense—though most people do many social things without reflecting very much about them. In the modern world a folkway is apt to be a cultural artifact—the conscious instrument of human will and purpose. **Often (and increasingly today) it is also the deliberate contrivance of a cultural elite.**

Gigwork is evolving from a narrowly scoped alternative mode of work into a full-blown folkway that fits Fischer's definition. Fischer used the concept of a folkway, in his classic *Albion's Seed*,[1] to talk about the early streams of immigration from Britain that made America what it is today. I have found it a useful concept for thinking about migrations in general, including conceptual ones across non-physical borders. For example, I've explored the idea of folkways of globalization[2], to think about the nature of our emerging cosmopolitan, globalized life (which is still evolving steadily, despite some reactionary backsliding). In fact, I'd argue that the gig economy is one of the major folkways of globalization.

What we are exploring here in this book, and what we are all doing in our respective corners of the gig economy, constitutes one stream of migration from an Old World—the industrial paycheck economy conforming to the contours of nation-state geography—to a New World, based on gigwork as a central economic mode, and conforming to the contours of global digital geography.

But to make the migration successful (which means nudging it to evolve into a full folkway by Fischer's definition, one that plays a significant role in shaping the future of the economy at large), significant injections of imagination and creative construction are required. Though they are primarily emergent phenomena, folkways don't make themselves. Per Fischer, they are the "deliberate contrivance of a cultural elite." And in the very young modern gig economy, merely surviving for a few years without descending into penury makes you part of the elite. Which means you bear a share of the responsibility for this deliberate contrivance.

Fischer lists the following components of a folkway, of which only *one* is about work *per se*: speech ways, building ways, family ways, gender ways, sex ways, child-rearing ways, naming ways, age ways, death ways, religious ways, magic ways, learning ways, food ways, dress ways, sport ways, *work ways*, time ways, wealth ways, rank ways, social ways, order ways, power ways and freedom ways.

Fischer's inventory is effectively a to-do list of social, cultural, and economic construction work that all of us in the gig economy participate in. Some of us do it consciously, others do it unconsciously, via casual advice they hand out, joking, griping and moaning on Twitter, and tips and tricks they borrow from peers.

It is tempting to think of this to-do list as an institution-building imperative, but that's too narrow. Though a folkway is a set of institutions in the broadest sense, when most people talk of institutions for the gig economy, they mean things like unions, coworking spaces, and health insurance.

That's not only too limited, it's a case of thinking ineffectively about the new through the lens of the old. Things aren't going to improve unless we in the gig economy take a *much* broader view of our responsibility for inventing our thread of the future for ourselves.

If we wallow in nostalgia for creaky, century-old constructs, all we'll do is reproduce old models with cosmetic tweaks, and undermine the gig economy rather than strengthen it. This tendency is often encouraged by people who are either not part of the gig economy, or don't want to be. Far too much of the conversation around the gig economy is driven by people who seem to be wishing it would just go away.

The idea of a folkway is an invitation to think more expansively and imaginatively, and go beyond formal cargo-cult institutions that mimic industrial paycheck economy institutions. This means thinking in more fluid ways about a much broader class of concerns. Everything ranging from handshakes and greetings—which are institutions by certain definitions—to games, mythologies, histories, and epistemologies. Otherwise we'll be eternally caught in the purgatory between predatory politicians, wannabe union organizers, and apathetic paycheck-employee-centric HR and purchasing departments.

We've barely scratched the surface here. While swapping tips and case studies and how-to playbooks for landing clients is valuable, it is not enough.

Two decades into the modern gig economy, constructing our identities primarily in terms of how we relate to the paycheck folkway is no longer good enough. After all, there is a good chance the gig economy will outgrow the paycheck economy, relegating the latter to a minority sector of the economy overall. Imagining our future in relation to the future of paycheck work would be like early industrial-age workers imagining their future in terms of the future of farming. Much of the supposed "future of work" thinking I see around the gig economy strikes me as the equivalent of early factory workers worrying about where to park their cows.

So the gig economy needs to outgrow its origin story in the paycheck world. For it to grow from limited sideshow to full-blown folkway, we need to talk about a lot more, and develop much deeper internal realities and subjectivities.

This process of reimagining and refactoring our world from an internal perspective is already underway. For example, people have lately been talking about the passion economy[3] as the evolutionary descendant of the gig economy. Nice development of a rudimentary inner life, but evolution can't stop at incorporating a notion of "passion." That's merely one more dimension. There are a couple dozen more to go before we can call ourselves a folkway.

There's a lot more evolving and designing and contriving to be done here, and by the time we are done, you and I will be old, and looking forward to whatever the equivalent of retirement is for the gig economy folkway (gigway?).

It's a long journey ahead, and we're just getting started.

---

1. www.amazon.com/Albions-Seed-British-Folkways-cultural/dp/0195069056
2. www.ribbonfarm.com/2010/06/16/the-missing-folkways-of-globalization/
3. See, for example, a16z.com/2019/10/08/passion-economy/.

SECTION THREE

BOOTSTRAPPING

The thing that is really hard, and really amazing, is giving up on being perfect and beginning the work of becoming yourself.

ANNA QUINDLEN

14

YOUR FIRST LEAP

EMPLOYEES HUNT, ENTREPRENEURS LAUNCH, GIGWORKERS LEAP

EMPLOYEES HUNT (or are headhunted) for jobs. Periodically. Every four years on average in the U. S. Entrepreneurs launch things. Serially. Winning big enough to stop with your first startup is very rare, as is stopping after your first success or failure.

Gigworkers? We leap into opportunity spaces. Not just once, but *repeatedly*. In the most extreme case, every new gig is a leap, and since you ideally have many gigs going in parallel, you are *always* leaping on some track. Sounds exhausting? It can be. But it need not be. And on the plus side, it can be exhilarating.

The first leap is special though, both in terms of significance in your life story, and in terms of the extra preparation it takes. The six chapters in this section are about taking a first leap into gigwork and retaining the goat-like leapiness indefinitely. It is primarily targeted at those of you who are either planning to make that first leap, or have already jumped and are failing at it. For those of you who have already made your first leap, this series should help improve your leaping habit, as you contemplate leap $n+1$, and also help you reflect more clearly on past leaps.

Leaping takes a very different kind of preparation than job-hunting or startup-launching, but it does have one thing in common with those other two kinds of starts/restarts: *it takes more scripting and preparation than you might think.*

Most people underprepare for job-hunting or startup-launching, but they tend to *wildly* underprepare for the gig-economy. Why? Because a gig economy has no default, ceremonial starting point. No initial focus of attention to get you started.

To prepare for a job search, you update your resume, search job sites, and let your friends know you are looking. To prepare for a startup launch, you brainstorm ideas, make prototypes and prepare pitch decks. Even if these activities aren't quite the right things to be doing, they do get you thinking about preparedness, and you might bootstrap from those formulaic behaviors to more imaginative preparations that work better. But there's no such obvious ceremonial starting point for scripting a leap into the gig economy. Only a joke one—getting business cards.

Well, actually, there *is* one real starting point: getting and staying married to someone with a job, who is willing to support your risk-taking and backstop your first leap with their own stability.[1] But this is obviously not a decision you should make *solely* to hedge against the risks of leaping into the gig economy.

Also, three factors are making marriage less of a hedge against gig-economy risks. *First*, jobs are turning equally if not more risky. *Second*, there is a much higher chance than you might think of both of you wanting to make a move at the same time, often triggered by parallel behaviors like moving to a new city. In my case for instance, my wife quit her job and took a new one right around when I took my first leap.

Third, more and more people are making their first leaps into the gig economy very young, long before they consider getting married. I made my first leap at age 37, nearly six years after I got married, and after fifteen years in the paycheck world. Many gig-economy aspirants I meet this days seem to be leaping in right after college or high school, and at least a decade before they are likely to get married, if they ever do.

Bottomline, most people never script their first leap at all. So their unprepared leaps turn fatal (too often, literally). This happens via three mistakes.

THREE MISTAKES AND A FUNERAL

The first mistake you can make in launching a gig economy career is to think it is pure improvisation. Movies and TV shows encourage this misconception by portraying characters who quit in a huff after some last straw, some final unbearable assault on their dignity or values, and just make it work somehow. Think Jerry Maguire, or Michael Scott in *The Office* declaring, "You have no idea how high I can fly!"

The second mistake you can make is thinking the kind of scripting that works for job-searching will also leave you prepared for the gig economy as a bonus. After all, a gig economy career is just a series of temporary jobs or a *I-am-the-product* startup, right? Wrong. The third mistake you can make is to treat the gig economy as a natural and predefined Plan B you automatically land in if you fail at the other two. As though nature has very kindly arranged the gig economy as a backup safety net. This idea has become *just* true enough in recent years (thanks to gig platforms in particular) that it can be the worst mistake of all, since it can suck you into down-wardly mobile trajectories.

Most people manage to make all three mistakes at once, and as a result, don't so much leap into a gig career as crash unceremoni-ously into one, against their will, having exited a job or other seem-ingly safe situation with nowhere near enough logistical or psychological preparation. How do you think that turns out?

ANATOMY OF A CRASH

Crash-landers almost never fare well enough to last. They limp along, getting physically and psychologically battered, until they

either get back into a job (often a worse job taken out of despera-
tion), or find a stable but unhappy situation as a dependent (via
reluctant parents or a resentful spouse).

And many never make it at all. Unplanned crashes into the gig
economy can go so badly, suicide is unfortunately a way out that
many choose.[2] It is a particularly severe risk for men. If leapers
survive and crawl back into the job economy, from the vantage
point of failure, they help amplify the unfounded belief that the gig
economy is an utterly unpredictable and precarious Hobbesian
wilderness where you have to be a lucky, unprincipled, mercenary
hustler-barbarian to survive. This is just plain false.

With the right preparation, the gig economy is no more risky or
uncivilized a place to be than the modern paycheck economy or the
entrepreneurial economy. The risks are just differently distributed,
require different patterns of preparation prior to the first leap, and
different ongoing risk-management behaviors. There are two
broad subsets of preparation required: inner and outer, which I'll
cover in the next few chapters.

---

1. And you might have to reciprocate in the future if you want to be a gigworking
   couple.
2. www.menshealth.com/health/a19533897/unemployment-suicide-risk/

15

LEAP RISK

THE MATH OF A SUCCESSFUL AND SAFE LEAP INTO FREE AGENCY

IN THE PREVIOUS CHAPTER, we looked at the anatomy of the first leap into the gig economy. We looked at why people tend to fail at it by being underprepared in multiple ways. The lack of an obviously meaningful ceremonial starting point, like preparing a resume, pitch deck, or prototype, makes the problem worse. So even though the risk, *properly managed*, is not significantly higher than a job search or entrepreneurial venture (lower actually, for people with ambiguous and/or low-demand skills), the outcomes are probably worse because of these under-preparation factors.

How do you prepare? Let me give you a starting point that is both useful preparation and a good ceremonial starting point: computing your *unmanaged leap risk*, as illustrated in the diagram on the next page. Our goal with this exercise is to first estimate your *income replacement horizon* (in months) and from that, your *unmanaged leap risk* (in dollars). Let's make up acronyms for these, why not: IRH and ULR.

Income Replacement Horizon (IRH) is the transitional period you might have to endure to get back to your pre-leap lifestyle quality. There Will be a Dip. Your first leap is generally a planned economic recession in your personal life. The better you prepare, the shorter and shallower it will be.

Unmanaged Leap Risk (ULR) is the dollar value of the strategic cleverness you *must* bring to your leap to *manage* unmanaged risk. I call it *minimum-viable cunning.* MVC. Without MVC you won't be able to close the strategy gap required for a successful first leap and, barring a big stroke of dumb luck, you'll end up in a traumatic crash that might scare (and scar) you out of the gig economy for life.

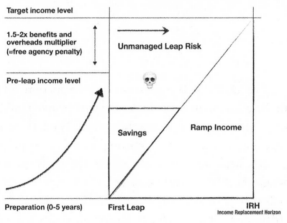

| Compute your *Unmanaged Leap Risk*

In other words, the estimation model assumes you'll be *doing* something meaningful to manage the unmanaged risk, not just sitting around, *and that you will be successful.* If you leave it unmanaged or fail despite trying to manage it, the model breaks. We plan for success not because it is guaranteed, but because it is the only thing you *can* tractably plan for. Failure is much messier than success, and planning for it doesn't actually help much (in fact it can hurt), so why bother? Here's an estimation example. It is meant to be illustrative, not definitive, and you have to get good at making up such rough models on your own.

1. Current monthly pre-tax salary: $5,000 aka $60,000/year
2. Adjust with 1.5x benefits/overhead multiplier—generic job, generic benefits, no special infrastructure: $7,500/month aka $90,000/year
3. Ramp length: divide by 10k, multiply by 4 = 36 months/3 years. *This is IRH.*
4. Unchanged-lifestyle income needed till IRH: $7,500 x 36 = $270,000
5. Average ramp income % assumption till IRH: 50%
6. Perfect nominal safety savings target: 36 months x $7,500 x 50% = $135,000
7. Actual savings at first leap: $35,000
8. Unmanaged leap risk: $135,000–$35,000 = $100,000. *This is ULR.*

In other words you're taking a risky leap worth $100,000 in strategic cleverness if you make it. Take a look at the image to get a visual sense of this model. The basic idea behind this computation is derived from job searching, but drastically modified. In job searching a common heuristic is that you can expect to look for a job for one month for every $10,000 in income. So a $60,000 job means six months of looking (and therefore having up to six months worth of savings for the most conservative preparation).

The equivalent rule of thumb for a gig economy launch is that you can expect four months of ramping for every $10,000 in paycheck income (benefits-and-overheads-adjusted) you want to replace with gig income. That same $60,000 income (worth $90,000 including benefits-and-overheads value) will take thirty-six months to replace rather than six.

The benefits-and-overheads value of a paycheck job is something like a free-agency penalty because you have to make up for it on your own, often paying a higher direct and/or hidden cost.

If you were in a basic, generic-skills job, the multiplier of about 1.5 accounts for having to provide for yourself the basic amenities that jobs generally provide. Like health insurance (in the U.S.), a retirement plan with matching, a computer loaded up with generalized and specialized productivity software, support from staff functions like accounting and administration, and, most importantly, *invisible perks like easily getting a lease or mortgage (via employers underwriting the risk of landlords renting to you or banks lending to you by guaranteeing your income)*.

How much in savings do you need before you make your first leap? Assuming a linear gig income ramp as shown in the diagram (optimistic; it's more likely to be an S-curve where you draw down savings faster in the beginning), you can assume that about half your income needs in the interim will be met by live earnings. Revise this upwards or downwards depending on how in-demand your skills/services are.

So a 36-month replacement horizon for a 60k job with a 1.5x multiplier amounts to about $270,000 as an income planning target, assuming no downward adjustment in lifestyle. If you expect to meet half of this, or $135,000, with ramping income, you'll need $135,000 to make the leap with complete safety and no significant lifestyle risks.

But obviously, trying to hit 135k in liquid savings on a 60k salary is ridiculously unrealistic for most people. At a very aggressive savings rate of say 20%, *above and beyond retirement savings,* it would still take you ten years to prepare to leap. You'd effectively never do it if you're that risk-averse.

A good way to think of this is in terms of a time advantage. You're hoping to make up for this 10-year-long, dumb, no-risk preparation time with sheer strategic cleverness. You're trying to leap ten years into your own financial future somehow. You're trying to disrupt yourself.

You'll leap with much less than the "safe" amount. You'll take a risk and bet on your own resourcefulness. In the example, I've assumed 35k in savings, leaving 100k unaccounted for. This difference is a measure of your ULR.

If ULR is zero, you're not taking enough risk, or equivalently, you're waiting too long to leap. But if you're not doing some cunning strategery to *manage* this risk with levers *besides* more saving or drawing down other assets (second mortgage, borrowing against retirement account), you're not being strategic enough. In other words, you need to take on pretty high unmanaged leap risk, equivalent to a year or two of your current income, and then *manage it* using things other than money.

There are four main cheats for managing the risk: favorable exit conditions, a parental factor, a spousal factor, and a transient life-style cost-down (a *permanent* cost-down is not a strategic move; it is a values shift towards frugality or a cheaper "lifestyle design" in Bali). Without cheats to manage it, the unmanaged risk part translates to an expectation of pain. Like homelessness pain. Or hunger pain. Or credit-card-debt pain. Or compounding-health-issues pain. Or tanking-mental-health pain. Or being-a-burden-on-friends-and-family pain. Or marriage-breaking-up pain. Or children-taken-away-by-social-services pain. Or doing-without-vacations pain. Or cutting-back-on-lattes pain.

You're not a masochist. You don't want to experience *any* of this pain. And if you plan right, you may not have to. Chances are you won't get out of Ramping Jail free, but you can minimize the pain. Your lifestyle pain tolerance may be high for merely staying alive, but to make a gig economy leap work, you can't be in extreme, chronic lifestyle pain. You need a relatively clear head and a couple of latte treats a week. And there are no dignity prizes for handling homelessness or untreated diabetes well.

So don't be a hero. Cheat. Figure out a way to cover the unmanaged leap risk, or ULR, with things other than money. Conjure up the minimum-viable cunning somehow. Next we'll look at cunning plans for doing this.

16

MINIMUM-VIABLE CUNNING

HOW TO INJECT ENOUGH STRATEGY INTO YOUR FIRST LEAP TO MANAGE THE LEAP RISK

LET'S TALK ABOUT CHEATS: unfair advantages and cheap tricks that, deployed with imagination and cunning, might mitigate a lot of the unavoidable unmanaged risk of leaping into the gig economy. I call these mechanisms *cheats* because they are not part of a general theory of systematic risk management. They are situational factors, likely unique to you, for making the leap in a particular place at a particular time. Your cheats come together in *your* pattern of what I call *minimum-viable cunning*.

I'm going to discuss four common cheat cards that apply to most people. You can and should think through and identify any uncommon cheat cards available to you.

| Common cheat cards

In *Your First Leap*, I set the stage by distinguishing the leap into the gig economy from job searches and entrepreneurial ventures and identifying common underpreparation mistakes that lead to a lot of people crashing and burning and returning to the paycheck economy in a weakened state, scarred and scared out of the gig economy for life.

In *Leap Risk*, I walked you through a rough estimation process to get a sense of the risk of your leap and how much of it is unmanaged. Roughly speaking, you can expect about four months of ramping to replace every $10,000 (or the equivalent in your country, if you're not in the U.S.) of fully loaded paycheck income. Optimistically, you can expect to make about half of your income during the ramping phase from gigs. In the example we worked out, $60,000 in annual income led to thirty-six months (three years) of ramping to replace with gig income and an unmanaged risk estimate of about $100,000 during that period which you can think of as an income gap you don't yet know how you'll fill.

We concluded that you're unlikely to be able to close the risk gap purely through additional savings because it would take too much time. That's why you need cheats, cunningly deployed. In fact, even if you *could* close the gap with money, you probably shouldn't. Figuring out how to close risk gaps with cunning rather than money is essential early training in gig economy resourcefulness. Because remember: the gig economy is not a single leap, but *repeated* leaping. You have to learn to be a goat. If you make it too easy on yourself, you'll never learn the necessary goat skills. Let's look at the four common cheats, in increasing order of importance: the spouse factor, the parent factor, the transient cost-down factor, and the exit conditions factor.

THE SPOUSE FACTOR

I already briefly talked about the huge effect being married or in a committed long-term relationship has on leaps into the gig economy.

Even if you're currently single, this is an aspect you should wrap your head around because it may be a factor in leaps beyond your first one.

The example I worked out last time was for a single person or single-earner household. It's harder to model a double-income couple's finances, and even harder if you have kids. But there's an upside to that complexity: a double-income couple can generally get by on a single income almost indefinitely with sufficiently aggressive austerities. Why? Because people tend to marry or partner-up within their own economic class, and even if one spouse earns much more, the lifestyle tends to be baseline affordable by one alone. At least for a while. You may have to slum it out at the bottom of your social class or move down a rung, but you'll live.

But as I noted in previous chapters, getting married solely to enable gig economy participation is a terrible idea. It's actually kinda like getting married to get a green card or visa. In both cases, it can be a great bit of free upside if you want to get married anyway, but a fatal flaw in the plan if you don't. And while a financially stable partner can be a great asset, you also have to be on the lookout for the possibility that *both* of you might have to make leaps at about the same time. This is likely beyond random chance.

To make *your* leap work out, you might have to do something like move to a cheaper city, which might force a complementary leap for your partner too. In my case, my wife quit her job within a couple of months of me making my leap, in part because of conditions created by my move. She did get a new one shortly after, but for a brief period, we were in a pretty dicey situation.

But with all those caveats in place, if you are married, that fact can either be a huge strategic advantage or a major liability (amounting to divorce-grade stress) depending on how the two of you pool your strategic options. The advantages can range from the small but important things like switching health insurance or getting a lease on the strength of your partner's income, to big ones like managing a long ramping period of lowered income.

Even if your partner does not work, they will likely be playing a major defensive role. As earner, you play offense and bring in the money. But managing a household budget on a volatile gig income, especially during a ramp phase, is vastly more complex than managing it on a paycheck. Everything from strategic prioritization of spending to being very savvy about sales and coupons is worth real money. If your non-working partner has the right mindset for playing defense, they may be able to squeeze $1.50—$2.00 in value out of every $1 you bring in. They may be able to basically sustain the same lifestyle you were used to, at a steep discount, simply by being smarter about spending money. A good defense partner is a major force multiplier.

You could do this for yourself of course, but remember, every cycle of brain time you spend playing defense you're not playing offense, so it is hugely valuable to have somebody else take care of that, allowing you to focus on the top line rather than the bottom line. Also, in my experience, playing offense and playing defense require very different mindsets that are rarely found in the same person, but are often found in a couple.

And finally, don't forget: your partner is likely going to be one of the only sources of skills and support you might need that you don't have to pay for with cash upfront. Chances are, they will not be actually interested in doing things you need done, and might not be particularly good at it, but they will likely do it anyway to support you, while you spin up the means to pay for the services from external sources. Your partner might end up as your unpaid bookkeeper, web designer, spreadsheet wrangler, or copyeditor. And you will likely be reciprocating in the future, underwriting their risks.

The great thing is that partners who support each other through leaps into free agency will likely grow together strongly as couples and the relationship will benefit. After eldercare and parenting, it's probably the richest shared growth experience you can have in a marriage. Of course, handled wrong, it can end in disaster, full of mutual resentment.

Factor in those options in making your plans. It is up to you whether your partner becomes your secret weapon or someone who weighs you down and turns the leap into a crash. To enjoy the former outcome rather than suffer the latter, you must make them a full partner in your leap. A part of the solution rather than a part of the problem. If you cannot, then you must rethink either the leap or the relationship.

THE PARENT FACTOR

Even if you're quite old, chances are your parents can help in at least a small way. They may be able to give you some money outright. Or you may be able to temporarily live with them. Or they may be able to co-sign an apartment lease with you if you can't show enough proof of income.

One particularly tough case I heard of was from a young Lyft driver, a Filipino immigrant. He was driving Lyft because his wife had died, leaving him to care for a young infant by himself. He had to quit his job in security work, which did not allow him the flexibility to handle childcare, and had to make things work another way. So he moved in with his mother-in-law and she let him use her car to make money driving for Lyft, while she handled some of the childcare. He was taking ESL and computer classes at night to level up into something better.

That's a pretty rough leap into the gig economy. One that could have gone far worse without a parent factor.

Don't be snobby about parental support. Your parents' generation probably didn't have to try making it *en masse* in the gig economy, so give yourself a break, courtesy of your parents (or in-laws), if you can. Intergenerational wealth transfer is a major dynamic in civilized life and most parents are more than willing to help as much as they are able. Historically, parents in the U.S. helped their children by contributing to a down payment for a mortgage, thereby enabling early home ownership. Helping you launch a gig-economy career is the same thing.

Of course not all parents are great parents, and support might come with strings attached or abuse. Be wary of disempowering false narratives, snide remarks about "getting a real job" and "when I was your age, XYZ," (especially if you're leaping into the creative or artistic side of the gig economy), and general undermining of what you're doing. And be aware that this is something parents can do unconsciously, without intending to, while still sincerely believing they're being loving and supportive.

It's not actually a strategic cheat if you have to pay for material support with your mental health. This risk of undermining is present in the spouse factor too, but is often easier to manage, in part because you choose your partner, but not your parents.

THE TRANSIENT-COST-DOWN FACTOR

In our leap risk model, we came up with a risk estimate based on the assumption that lifestyle would remain constant.

Chances are, you *won't* maintain the lifestyle, but will be able to execute a planned, transient lifestyle cost-down with little to no loss of living standards. Moving to a cheaper apartment in a cheaper city is often the biggest piece of the cost-down puzzle. If you nail that, the rest falls into place. If you screw that up, other economies may not add up to enough. If you're single and have a particularly mobile gig economy strategy, moving overseas to a cheaper operating location is an extreme version of this cost-down move. That playbook has been done to death, so I won't belabor it.

When I quit, we landed in Las Vegas because my in-laws have a home there, which they left vacant anyway during the summers. For six months, we paid them a small rent that was one-fifth our Washington, D.C. rent, a sweet deal for both sides. Then we moved into an apartment that was one-third the cost of our apartment in the D.C. area. That was a *big* cheat for a while (a combination parent cheat and cost-down cheat). When we moved to Seattle a year later, we returned to paying roughly D.C.-level rents. But the Vegas leg of my ramping period was a crucial strategic cheat. I estimate it was worth nearly $35,000 in saved rent alone, relative to our D.C. or Seattle lifestyle. We basically did a cost-of-living gravity slingshot through Las Vegas, between east and west coasts.

Be careful though: it's easy to end up fetishizing frugal living, especially if both members of a couple are better at playing defense than offense, and letting the transient cost-down turn permanent. It's fine if that's what you were aiming for all along, and there are websites and mailing lists out there to help you with that. But here at the Art of Gig, we are solving for a non-minimalist, non-spartan lifestyle: just on your own terms rather than those of a paycheck employer.

If you are in the U.S., health insurance can be another big shock if you've never paid for fully loaded healthcare. The cost of COBRA (opt-in continuation of employer health insurance up to 18 months after quitting a job) or ACA may be between 3–5x the payroll deduction you're used to. So you may have to make cuts in other areas to maintain the same or worse healthcare. Other countries mostly have more sane and gig-economy-friendly healthcare systems, but have other headaches. No country in the world is entirely friendly to free agency. We live in a world designed around paychecks. Understand the difference that makes to the cost of living and plan your cost-down accordingly.

A transient cost-down is a non-trivial bit of planning, so don't wing it. If you don't have at least a couple of spreadsheets going to figure it out, you're doing it wrong.

THE EXIT CONDITIONS FACTOR

The biggest cheat in making a successful leap? It isn't when or where you leap, but what you leap *with*. What are your assets? What are you carrying in that big figurative bundle in your arms when you make the leap? The things in that bundle constitute your exit conditions. This is one cheat card you *must* play. The other things can be optional or unavailable to you, but exit conditions are something you can always design at least a little bit.

The worst exit conditions are: getting blindsided by being laid off or fired with no severance, when you are under immense cash flow pressure or debt, perhaps dealing with family emergencies, and being forced to make the leap empty-handed. Good outcomes are unlikely there, but if you're ever in that situation, I wish you luck with it. But if you can do better than that, and not exit empty-handed, your chances improve dramatically. Some exit conditions are what I think of as *low-cunning* exit conditions:

- If you can time your first leap from a job at an old, declining company with a voluntary-retirement scheme, sweet. Grab that exit condition with both hands.
- If layoffs are being planned, with generous severance packages, and you can maneuver to be on the list, go for it. You may not be one of the people they want to lose, but if they have to meet specific headcount-cut targets, they'll be open to it.
- If you can exercise good employee perks just before you leave, like getting subsidized software, do so. If your employer is folding and you get first shot at snagging used assets for free or cheap, like office furniture or valuable bits of intellectual property, go for it.
- If you have to wait a few months for some stock options or RSUs to vest, go ahead and wait, but not too long; I walked away from a bunch because the vesting horizon was too far out.
- If you can get a new, cheaper apartment lease on the strength of your paycheck job just before you quit, do it.

Just be careful: don't let low-cunning exit-condition engi-neering turn into unprincipled or illegal behaviors. A typical gray-area case is "stealing" clients. You may be bound by a noncompete agreement, in which case it might be outright illegal. Even if it isn't illegal, it may cost you in burned bridges and relationships and reputational damage as people tag you as someone who pulls that sort of jerk move. Even if you are willing to take that damage, it might just be a shitty thing to do to other people who don't deserve it.

But there are also situations where taking clients from a job with you is both a norm in that industry and the best deal for all parties concerned. Just be thoughtful, and avoid hurting others in navigating this sort of thing.

Your main focus, however, should be on *high-cunning* exit conditions. That's the real test of your imagination. The best high-cunning exit condition is one in which you've created a live asset, out in the open, that can be turned into a viable foundation for a gig-economy business with the flip of a switch. In my case, all it took to flip the switch was a blog post declaring I was going free-agent and I instantly had a flood of live goodwill and support flowing towards me (including some sponsorship money, and a lead for what turned into a big gig a year later). Throw-a-switch leap assets are of three major kinds:

- *Marketing assets* like a blog or newsletter where you can start to look for and create opportunities. I had both.
- *Product assets* that can be turned into a money-making thing on Day 1. I had a nearly complete book that I was able to finish and put up for sale within a month of quitting. Instant spike of cash flow right when it was most useful.
- *Live, hot leads* that can be converted to starter gigs *before* you quit. I had two consulting gigs and a writing gig

lined up a month before I quit. They didn't amount to much, but having *any* cash flow going was a big deal.

An interesting point about the book: it was a premium exit condition for me because I was quitting Xerox, where I'd learned a lot about print-on-demand economics and the publishing industry. So I was able to self-publish my book in the most efficient, highest-margin way possible, and make serious money off it. Book publishing is great for reputation, but not generally a good way to make money unless you do it yourself and know what you're doing. In my case, I did know what I was doing, so the book was a significant chunk of my income throughout my ramp period, and still continues to make decent money today, over a decade later.

Keep a particular look out for this kind of premium exit condition: valuable knowledge or skills you've acquired in the run-up to the leap that you can deploy in ways most people cannot.

PUTTING IT TOGETHER

That's it for the four major cheat cards. Add any others you have ready to play. Put it all together, lay it all out on the table in front of you. Stare hard at what you have. Somewhere in there lies a cunning plan that can cover for your leap-risk deficit. Somewhere in there are thousands of dollars in risk-mitigation value. Hard, financial, cover-the-rent value, not vague soft-assets value. Somewhere in there is the key to leaping successfully *vs.* crashing and burning.

If you haven't yet made the leap, kudos for starting to think about it. Take a deep breath. Even with all the preparation in the world, it's going to be something of a shock to your system. You will gasp for breath. Your mammalian diving reflex will be activated, figuratively speaking. If you've already taken your first leap and survived, congrats. As you've no doubt already learned, there are no medals. Employees get employee-of-the-month awards. Startup founders get flattering media coverage and awards at conferences with pitch contests. But there are no prizes for making a successful leap into the gig economy. All you win is the opportunity to leap yet again. And again. And again. The reward for leaping is getting started on a learning curve that makes you better at leaping, putting you in touch with your inner goat.

The first leap into free agency and gigwork takes a lot of nerve and imagination, which is why most people get involuntarily dumped into it via layoffs or firings, and with a high chance of crashing and burning rather than making the leap deliberately, on their own terms, with vastly better outcome probabilities.

The *nerve* part lies in making the leap without having a complete answer to the question of how you're going to make it work. The *imagination* part lies in pulling together the minimum-viable cunning needed to make it work, using the cheat cards you have available to you. In these last three chapters, I've outlined a basic approach to taking your first leap. Together, the ground we've covered so far constitutes what you might call the outer game of leaping. All the practical stuff. In the next chapter, we'll cover what I think of as the inner game: preparing your mindset and mental models for leap conditions. The *really* practical stuff.

17

THE INNER GAME OF GIGWORK

BECOMING MORE OF A ROBOT TO EXPRESS MORE OF YOUR HUMANITY

IN THE LAST THREE CHAPTERS, we explored the first leap into the gig economy, leap risk, and minimum-viable cunning. Together, these topics cover what you might call the *outer* game of gigwork. The practical stuff.

Continuing this 101 series, this time, I want to tackle what I think of as the *inner* game of gigwork. The *really* practical stuff. The inner work you need to do to ensure your new life is a more enriching, high-agency life that allows you to be more fully human than the life you're leaving (or contemplating leaving) behind. Ironically, the key to doing this is seeing yourself as more of a robot.

YOU, ROBOT

If a job is a simple plastic mask that hides the "real you" who comes out on evenings and weekends, a gigwork identity is an entire robot suit that allows you to *express* the real you. Lifestyle design is robot design. Weird, huh? It's the paradox of the inner game.

The more you can get comfortable in a robotic skin, for a precise sense of *robotic* that I'll get to, the more human you can be. The more you resist and hold on to an egoistic sense of your own humanity, the more you'll be reduced by circumstances to a low-agency precious-snowflake zombie at the mercy of the environment. In the economic outer space that is the gig economy, your robot suit is also a spacesuit that allows you to survive. Your choice of personas, on the surface, can seem like it's between being a human non-playable character or a high-agency robot character.

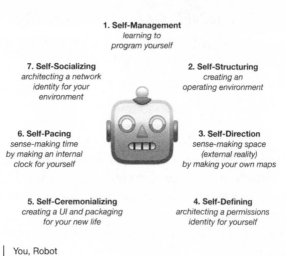

1. Self-Management
*learning to
program yourself*

7. Self-Socializing
*architecting a network
identity for your
environment*

2. Self-Structuring
*creating an
operating environment*

6. Self-Pacing
*sense-making time
by making an internal
clock for yourself*

3. Self-Direction
*sense-making space
(external reality)
by making your own maps*

5. Self-Ceremonializing
*creating a UI and packaging
for your new life*

4. Self-Defining
*architecting a permissions
identity for yourself*

| You, Robot

The key to unraveling the paradox is understanding that in the paycheck economy you're *already* a robot but you're just not aware of it. In the gig economy, you just have to become aware of and own that fact. And if you own it well, you'll appear more intensely human to others, the opposite of robotic.

In the gig economy, you're insourcing a lot of the robotic aspects of your being that were previously embedded in your workplace environment, and now have to be part of your life environment. In both cases, what they do is create a container for your squishy, messy, human psyche. In the process of insourcing, you'll be personalizing and customizing to yourself, so you'll be more free to express yourself. Recognizing this is what dissolves the paradox.

To extend our robots-spacesuits analogy, paycheck employees

are also robots. They just don't realize it because their robot suit is a large shared spaceship containing a lot of people in a single life-support environmental system. The interior fosters an illusion of greater humanity than they actually possess. Being in a robot spacesuit simply brings the reality of economic outer space so close to you that the illusion breaks. But your spacesuit is still more human-shaped than the spaceship.

INNER GAME VS. OUTER GAME

The title of this chapter is a hat-tip to an excellent book, Timothy Gallway's *Inner Game of Tennis*—not directly relevant to our subject matter here, but a generally good read on developing a creative mindset. It too has a curiously robot-design approach to its subject. Turns out, the key to getting into a zen-like mindset while playing tennis has to do with short-circuiting your ego so you can relate to yourself as a sensorimotor machine that plays tennis.

The inner game of gigwork is much simpler than the outer game, but much harder. The outer game has a lot of messy and complicated details. A lot of logical puzzles to figure out, non-trivial budget arithmetic, and timing and strategy challenges to solve. But if you're moderately smart, none of it is actually hard, just tedious. The math is not genius-level math. The chess-like strategy elements do not require grandmaster-level skill to work out and play out. The complicated details are more like Ikea furniture assembly than neurosurgery. And none of it requires extreme precision. You can kinda half-ass a lot of it and figure it out as you go along.

The outer game is forgiving so long as you're paying attention and thinking, and willing to change what you're doing as you learn. The inner game though, despite being much simpler in terms of number of moving parts, is really hard. And it is less forgiving. If you manage your psyche wrong through a critical period, it might be the end.

THE CASE FOR FLYING BLIND

Preparing for the inner game is preparing for the evolution of your own psyche through the first few years as you ramp into the gig economy. It is predicting your own emotional reactions and preparing yourself to regulate them in helpful ways. You can't tell how you'll react to your first serious cash-flow panic, but with the right inner-game disciplines in place, it is more likely to be a good reaction. But before I outline that preparation process, I want to touch on the case for *not* preparing. Unlike the outer game, where underpreparation has clear risks and downsides, in the inner game, the benefits of preparing *vs.* not preparing are less clear.

Why? The inner game is hard enough that you could argue the best way to tackle it is to not even realize how hard it is before diving in, and then working it all out under live-fire conditions. Then you can look back and marvel at your own survival. There's a certain gonzo poetry to that kind of outcome: clueless newbies not knowing a problem is impossible according to more experienced people and solving it anyway. It's the stuff of legend.

This approach might even lead to *better* results sometimes. If you don't read articles or books about the gig economy which try to prepare you for what you're getting yourself into, you might pull off some inspired blank-sheet creativity. That said, I do think survivorship bias in the narratives of these survivors tends to blind us to the fates of those who *don't* make it, and who perhaps might have with a little bit more conscious mental preparation.

On balance, I think it is better to look ahead at what to expect for your inner journey. You might end up doing things a little less imaginatively, but you lower your risk of not making it. It's a worthwhile trade-off. A possible outcome of going through such mental self-preparation is that you might decide you're *not* psychologically up to the challenge, reassess the true value of a paycheck job, and decide that's a better fit for you after all. And that's okay.

That's great. The more you consciously choose the roles you're cast into, the better you fit them.

If the only thing I achieve in this chapter is making some of you happier about your jobs and more content to stay in them, that would be a good outcome. A better outcome would be if more people left unsatisfying paycheck jobs for more satisfying gig economy careers, and did it well enough to make it.

BUILDING ROBOT *SELF-X*

Setting up to play a good inner game is, like I said, not complicated. It's just hard. All of the inner game can be summarized as building a *SELF-X* system. Where *X* is any kind of primarily psychological support that used to be provided for you by coworkers, managers, or leaders in an employer organization (or in the case of fresh graduates, a university campus and parental support). *SELF-X* is also a nice name for a robot suit. The inner game is doing for yourself all the psychological environment maintenance work *X* that used to be invisibly done for you.

I'm going to lay it out for you in the form of an inventory of inner-game competency areas (or in our allegory, robot design areas) to think about and figure out. Get your expectations straight: You won't figure it all out at once. You'll iterate through approaches on all these fronts as your new life comes together via trial and error. Don't be a perfectionist about any of this. Just pick a starting design and iterate from there. I'm going to use the context of a regular job to describe all the *X*'s, but if you're a student who has not worked a full-time job before, substitute the university or school environment equivalents.

SELF-MANAGEMENT

When you are in a job, you are unaware of the extent to which you rely on other people to *manage* you. You take and hand out action items, you sit in meetings run according to certain protocols, you take responsibility for certain processes and systems, and so on. Jobs come with management structures that install behavioral code in you, which then runs to accomplish the work of the organization. Some workplaces are built around annual planning and goal setting. Others are built around corporate habits like agile development. Still others navigate via mission statements and manifestos. All vary in *how much* management they do (ranging from *laissez-faire* to micromanagement), but trust me, *all* of them manage you more than you realize, and you'll feel the management vacuum hard on Day 1.

In the gig-economy we have to learn self-management behaviors. How do you approach self-management? *Think of self-management as programming yourself like a robot.* This does not mean you have to be robotic in a stiff sense. You can be a gonzo robot like Bender on *Futurama*. You can be one of those Boston Dynamics gymnast robots. You can be a spunky little rover on Mars. But whatever your robot persona, it needs code to run. Code that used to come from others. If you don't give yourself code to run, you risk sitting there doing nothing. Seems obvious, but it's amazing how many people think being your own boss equals not *having* a boss. You won't magically be a better boss for yourself than other people were. There's a good chance you'll be worse at it. You have to learn how to be a good boss to yourself.

SELF-STRUCTURING

Self-structuring is subtly different. Most people need a certain amount of structure in their lives.[1] When the structure falls apart, they don't do well. As a gigworker, you have to build structure for yourself. Like building deliberate awareness of which Starbucks locations seem to foster what kinds of work moods for you. Like running experimental schedules to figure out whether you tend to work in 4-hour morning bursts or all-nighters. Like choosing whether to stock up a nice home office, rent a desk at a coworking space, or live out of a backpack. Like choosing a computer.

If you think your job is pretty flexible, think again. There are a thousand defaults that are set for you in *any* job. It doesn't have to be an industrial 9-to-5 job to serve as a strong forcing function on the structure of your work life.

How do you self-structure? *Think of self-structuring as creating an operating system around yourself.* Code needs an operating environment to run in. But unlike the self-management behavioral code you write to run the foreground of your work, the operating environment code is more likely to be assembled from multiple other sources. Your task is that of architectural selection, not construction. Though this might involve a lot of practical decisions like notebooks and computers and desks, they are primarily decisions that affect your inner mental state. That's why they're part of the inner game.

SELF-DIRECTION

You not only have to be managed in a job, you have to be *led,* which is an entirely different thing. To be managed is to be given behavioral code to run and an operating environment to run it in. Together, these determine *how* you work.

To be led is to be given a direction and motivation; a *why. Things to do and a reason to care.* I like A. G. Lafley's definition of leadership as "interpreting external reality for the organization." This is not an objective, dispassionate description, but an opinionated, emotional understanding that makes a particular direction of movement seem inevitable and aesthetically necessary, rather than merely logical.

Here's the thing: psychologically, it doesn't matter whether a leader is good or bad, whether their "interpretation of external reality" is a powerful vision or batshit insane or whether their direction is taking the company to the moon or over a cliff. The mere existence of any default interpretation of reality and direction of movement is enough to fill the need to be led. You'll just march along. Perhaps reluctant and grumbling, but you'll do it.

When you go free agent, you're on your own for this vectoring, and people tend to do badly without a sense of direction. They tend to stall entirely, and stop moving. As a result, one compensatory response is that free agents often fixate on what I call "free and open-source public leaders."

Charlie Munger for instance, is the *de facto* CEO of thousands of free agents. So are Paul Graham and Naval Ravikant. In a previous era, when the gig economy had a distinctly feminine tone to it due to the paycheck workplace being less friendly to women, Martha Stewart and Oprah Winfrey were the *de facto* CEOs for many women trying to run home-based businesses in the interstices of childcare and housework.

Admirable though such public leaders may be, they are *not actually your leader!* The only lasting solution is for you to become your own leader. Your own CEO. You interpret your own reality, you set your own direction. Inspired or insane, your own direction is the only one you'll be able to follow long-term.

Think of self-directing as making and maintaining your own maps, location awareness, and movement. Don't underestimate how hard it is. The easy part is drawing a map and picking a logically coherent direction to go. The hard part is doing it in a way that you'll actually care about going in that direction enough to take step after step, indefinitely. Orientation is more than location awareness. It is motivation. The words *motivation* and *motive* indicate an *urge* to movement, not merely a sense of direction.

SELF-DEFINING

In a job, who you are is determined by your job description and responsibilities. As a typical cynical employee, you might not care about titles and status beyond their link to compensation, perks and resume-stuffing for your next job. But even a title you're cynical about molds your sense of self at an unconscious level. If you say enough times to people, *I am Assistant Regional Manager at Dunder-Mifflin,* it *becomes* your self-definition. The mask becomes the person. One of the big effects is your role shapes your sense of agency.

In a gig economy, you have to do that for yourself. In my case, identifying as a "sparring partner" (see Section VI) was an important early step. Self-definition is not the same as self-classification. Things like 2x2s and taxonomies might help you self-classify, but self-definition is a declaration of who you are, and in particular, how you understand your own agency.

You're your own boss. What do you permit yourself to do? What rules that you used to follow in a paycheck job do you now break? What new rules do you now follow that you didn't before?

In our robot allegory, *self-definition is the act of constructing a permissions architecture around your own behaviors.* Think Asimov's Three Laws of Robotics. They aren't personal brands or logos. But they strongly define the nature of Asimovian robots. What are the laws of You, Robot? What does *doing the right thing* mean to you? What does *doing the thing right* mean to you? That's self-definition.

SELF-CEREMONIALIZING

Another thing that organizations give you is a sense of ceremonial appearance. A way you appear to others in the context of work. This is again far more important than you might think. So go ahead, order those business cards even if you have nobody to give them out to. Set up a website even if you have only uninspired boilerplate to put on it right now. Spend time cleaning up your LinkedIn. Have a friend take a couple of good headshots. Change your Twitter headline. Put your incorporation certificate up on the wall of your home office, even though nobody will ever come by to check. But don't go overboard into absurdity. Don't give yourself awards or silly titles even ironically. It's a waste of mental energy, and drains seriousness.

The point of self-ceremonialization is to close a sensory-cues feedback loop to manage your psyche. Think of it as setting up mirrors all around yourself, not out of vanity, but to reinforce a way of being. Some of this will happen naturally through self-structuring. An in-tray on your home office desk is both a ceremonial location for papers, and a cue to work on them. An *xkcd* cartoon on a cork board though, might not have any obvious cueing function for an instrumental behavior. It might just be an attitude set-point reminder or a reminder of some philosophical principle. That's part of the pure ceremony. The self-structured environment will get the work done, but it will likely not have the right emotional contours or signal the right priorities. Self-ceremonialization distorts the reality you inhabit in useful ways.

Think of it as taking the orienteering logic of self-direction, and the permissions architecture of self-definition, and using them to distort how the operating environment appears to you. Some things will loom larger, other things will shrink. Some things will be set up to be easier to do. Other things will be set up with guardrails to make them harder to do. The point is to make your new life *emotionally real* for yourself, by setting up your own reality-distortion field. *Think of self-ceremonializing as creating an effective UI for your new life.*

SELF-PACING

In a job, you have a reference pace or workplace tempo. You define your pace with reference to it. Do you go with the flow? Do you try to overtake others? Do you pace-set for others? Do you disrupt the flow?

In the gig economy, there is no default reference stream of activity for you to define your own pace against. Think about it. When you start, perhaps you have one client in Silicon Valley going crazy fast and another in a sleepy Midwestern town ambling along leisurely. Which one do you use as a reference?

Any simplistic reference-pacing will lead to schizophrenia. You have to look inward to develop your own sense of pace, relative to your own life. You have to create a time zone around yourself, just as ships out on the ocean have a shipboard time that is systematically set and reset as the ship sails across different longitudes.

How quickly do you respond to client emails? What does it mean when you promise someone something *as soon as possible*? What does "I'll get to it this week" actually mean when you say it? Does it mean the same thing when you say it to different clients?

In our robot allegory, *self-pacing is about sense-making in time via construction of an internal clock*, now that you don't have an external one from a workplace to drive you. It is actually another aspect of self-direction, the temporal dimension of leadership, but I like to break it out because it is a uniquely critical aspect.

The difference between armchair strategy and non-armchair live action often boils down to a ticking clock. The clock is the bridge between strategy and execution.

What is the right pace for the gig economy? It is almost always "faster than you are comfortable with." The environment will tempt you to its pace. As you move across contexts, you might start behaving like a temporal chameleon, relaxing with relaxed clients, going neurotic with neurotic clients. This is the dark side of "being on the clock" in metering and billing terms. If your clock is no more than the sum of billing clocks in your gigs, you've come temporally undone.

Don't come temporally undone. Build an inner clock. Set your own pace with reference to the state of your own inner game. One of the best ways to do this is to build up a compounding asset over time. Your internal clock is measurable by the runway you've laid out for yourself for that asset to gain value. For me, it's been writing about business topics. It's only a fraction of my writing, but it's obvious when I'm not moving at a decent clip: I don't have interesting new things to say on business topics. You could almost measure the pace of my consulting life by my rate of publishing decent business-related articles.

SELF-SOCIALIZING

The final part of your inner game setup is other people. In a job, there are typically cultural structures in place to socialize you into a role and keep you there, primarily via mediated interactions with other people. Happy hours, seminars, etc. In the gig economy, you have to do this to yourself. Hell is always other people, but as a gigworker you get to design your own hell. Make up a mix of social activities to suit your personality. Some mix of meetups, lunches with friends, and sessions at the coffee shop should do the trick.

You have to set up the social structure and cultural rhythms you need to function. That much is easy and obvious. The hard part of self-socializing is understanding how you depend on other people, who they are, and the extent to which they recognize the role they play in your new life, *and then rearranging things if they seem to be unhealthy and limiting rather than healthy and enabling.*

In a paycheck job, you don't have much control over who's in your socialization environment. In the gig economy you do. You can more easily cut out people who drag you down, and add people who lift you up. But it doesn't happen automatically. You have to exercise that capability to unlock a lot of the benefits of gigwork. But you'll be tempted to add and subtract exactly the wrong sorts of people, creating a self-defeating social environment for yourself. In our robot allegory, *self-socializing is architecting a network identity for your environment.*

PUTTING IT TOGETHER

Let's summarize. The inner game of gigwork is about constructing a robot suit for yourself, by insourcing things that used to be done for you, which help you manage your psyche as you figure out how to fend for yourself. There are seven basic areas of design to think about, as illustrated in the graphic at the beginning of this chapter.

1. *Self-Management:* Learning to program yourself
2. *Self-Structuring:* Creating an operating environment
3. *Self-Direction:* Sense-making external reality by making your own maps
4. *Self-Defining:* Architecting a permissions identity for yourself
5. *Self-Ceremonializing:* Creating a UI and packaging for your new life
6. *Self-Pacing:* Sense-making time by making an internal clock for yourself
7. *Self-Socializing:* Architecting a network identity for your social environment

This is a to-do list and a set of starter cues, with a hopefully helpful robot-spacesuit mixed metaphor. I'm not going to tell you *how* to set up your inner game. There's a lot of good and bad advice for all of these areas of design focus out there. How you put your mindset together by putting these robotic parts together, and how you breathe life into it by putting it on, is actually your first big challenge in the gig economy.

There's a holistic test for if it's working though. If you've designed your robot suit right, it should become almost invisible to both you and people who see you operating. You should feel a sense of freedom and control from the inside, and from the outside, exude a sense of intuitive agency. People may see you fumbling and stumbling. They may see you gracelessly working through trial-and-error experimentation. But they should get a sense that you know what you're doing.

If your robot suit is visible (in the form of formulaic behaviors that mark you as an easily identified "type" for instance, or as a "personal brand" robot that is put together with preternatural poise), it is a badly designed robot suit. Or the suit has become your master, like Doc. Ock's AI arms in Spider-Man. Many free agents in the internet marketing world unfortunately come across as bad robots, their humanity subordinated to a bad inner game that has has taken over their psyches. They look like characters out of a sketch comedy show rather than people. Parodies of themselves.

On the other hand, if you seem painfully all-too-human, but your behaviors seem whiny, overly vulnerable, and low-agency, you haven't in-sourced enough of your psychological support environment yet. Like a starving artist who produces no art, but is very loudly human about it, playing the part of a sensitive soul being tossed about by a cruel world. No, that's as bad as being a formulaic brand bot. That is performative learned helplessness. That's being a precious-snowflake zombie (I know I already said that, but I like that artistic slur so much, I had to repeat it ICYMI the first time).

Avoid both failure patterns. Get your inner game going right. Invisible suit, visible performance of real agency.

---

1. You can take a test known as the California Personality Inventory that will give you a sense of how much structure you need.

18

THE ROAD TO AGENCY

PUTTING TOGETHER THE WHOLE PLAYBOOK, AND MAKING THE LEAP

WITH THIS CHAPTER, we conclude our five-part series on leaping into the gig economy and put it all together with a preparation roadmap.

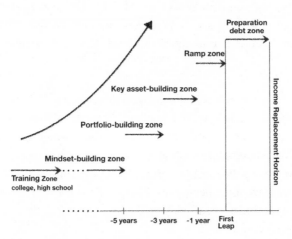

| Leaping into the gig economy

TIMING THE LEAP

Based on everything I've said so far in this section, about the first leap, leap risk, minimum-viable cunning, and the inner game of gigwork, you might be tempted to conclude you should look at the preparation work you have to do, and then plan to leap in *n* years, where *n* is a function of how much preparation you think you need.

No. This is exactly backwards. It's Soviet five-year plan thinking. It's corporate employee career-ladder thinking. You're not trying to put in the time to earn a desirable title or position like a corporate lifer. You're trying to craft an escape to free agency.

Illogical though it might sound, you have to *pick a date or leap event* (such as a certain critical meeting going a certain way), and then do the best job of preparation you can before that. The rest will have to be done under live-fire conditions *after* the leap.

Why? Because preparedness is actually the least important of four major factors that should influence the timing. It just happens to be the one you have most control over. The factors driving the timing of your leap are: *preparedness, risk appetite, opportunity,* and *depressors.* You can remember this with the convenient acronym PROD.

1. *Preparedness* is actually the least important of the four, but the only one you can actually do something about, so there is a temptation to let it drive the timing exclusively. I've written four posts about preparation, but that doesn't mean it's the most important factor in timing. I was very well-prepared personally, but that's just because my preparation needs happened to line up well with the right timing.

2. *Risk appetite,* in my experience, does not change much for people, barring seriously traumatic events (which in most cases reduces risk appetite rather than increasing it). While you can't change this, you can trick your risk

appetite in ways I will outline in the next section. I'm personally very risk averse in terms of financial and entrepreneurial risk, so I had to trick myself quite strongly.

3. *Opportunity* is the second most important factor, but the one least within your control. Y2K was a good example. It launched many companies and careers within a tight launch window. You can create small, local opportunities around yourself by taking the initiative, but the biggest tailwinds will generally be in the environment. You have to be alive to them. My opportunity was of course, the brief window of opportunity when blogs ruled the internet.

4. *Depressors* are the single most important factor. If you are in a situation you hate, doing work you dislike, with people you detest, in an industry you think is toxic and dying, everyday life becomes a kind of hell and you die a little more every day you stay there. If this applies to you (fortunately, it didn't apply to me), leap as soon as humanly possible, before you get reduced to subhuman gloom and there's not enough of you left to save.

Remember the acronym PROD: preparedness, risk appetite, opportunity, depressors. We've talked a lot about the first element in this series.

The last two are very situation-specific and I don't have much to say about the opportunities and depressors in *your* specific environment. If I had the bandwidth to offer 1:1 coaching, which I don't, this is what I'd spend a lot of time on. If you can find a friendly neighborhood gigworker who has already made the leap, you may want to seek out mentorship from them on opportunities and depressors.

The second element, *risk appetite*, is something we can say a few general things about.

HACKING RISK APPETITE

PROD gets at the logical, analytical side of timing the leap, but there's also a gut-level intuitive side to the timing, which involves hacking your risk appetite to accept the right level of risk rather than imposing the level of risk it is comfortable with on your conscious thought. Yeah, this is a mind-over-gut programming operation. Like messing with your gut microbiome with weird supplements.

And you *must* hack your risk appetite, otherwise it will trigger harmful stress responses that prevent you from managing the eminently manageable risks. You don't want to thrash and drown in two feet of water simply because you can't swim. Controlling your panic response will reveal the solution to be very simple: you don't need to learn to swim in five minutes. You just need to stand up.

There are two versions of risk-appetite hacking problems. Too much risk appetite (uncommon), and too little (much more common). Generally, too much risk appetite leads to leaping too early and too little risk appetite leads to leaping too late. Occasionally you see the reverse. Too much risk appetite leading to waiting too long (for the "big score" opportunity) and too little leading to leaping too early (because there's a less scary thing you can do now that's easier than waiting for the window of opportunity to do the more scary thing).

You don't want to be too early or too late. You want to time it *just right*. Don't underestimate the deep sense of power that comes from feeling in your gut that you're leaping at the right moment. Here's a famous dose of Shakespeare you should commit to memory:

> *There is a tide in the affairs of men.*
> *Which, taken at the flood, leads on to fortune;*
> *Omitted, all the voyage of their life*

Is bound in shallows and in miseries.
On such a full sea are we now afloat,
And we must take the current when it serves,
Or lose our ventures.

The more time you have available, the more (and more effectively) you can prepare—up to a point. Beyond that point, more preparation is actually fear. It might be valuable, but the value will be lower than the cost of missed opportunities, toll exacted by continuing in depressing situations, and not hacking your gut to take better risks. Here's a second dose of Shakespeare you should commit to memory:

Art thou afeard
To be the same in thine own act and valor
As thou art in desire? Wouldst thou have that
Which thou esteem'st the ornament of life,
And live a coward in thine own esteem,
Letting "I dare not" wait upon "I would,"
Like the poor cat i' th' adage?

These two verses, interestingly, are spoken by Brutus and Lady Macbeth, the villains of *Julius Caesar* and *Macbeth* respectively. The kind of boldness it takes to navigate your first leap is actually the same kind of boldness it takes to commit murder. Except in this case, the victim is your old low-agency, unhappy self rather than another person. You'll still be unhappy (happiness is overrated), but it will be an interesting new kind of high-agency unhappiness that you'll actually enjoy mastering. If only because you'll only have yourself to blame with pointy-haired bosses and toxic coworkers out of the equation.

Your first leap is an ego death triggered by out-of-comfort-zone risk-taking, followed by regeneration into a fuller life. You know in your gut you must leap, because to not do so would be to resign yourself to a slow death.

Once you've truly committed at gut level, you will find that waiting is almost intolerable, and you will *naturally* try to advance the timing. The risk of mistiming the leap will shift polarity. Where you previously risked procrastinating until it's too late, you will now risk leaping too soon because the stress of waiting is too much (the way nervous soldiers might fire before "seeing the whites of their eyes"). Shakespeare one more time, again from *Julius Caesar*.

> *Between the acting of a dreadful thing*
> *And the first motion, all the interim is*
> *Like a phantasma or a hideous dream.*
> *The genius and the mortal instruments*
> *Are then in council, and the state of a man,*
> *Like to a little kingdom, suffers then*
> *The nature of an insurrection.*

The point of developing an awareness of this gut-level aspect is not to change your risk appetite, but to hack it. That element of PROD, like I said, is not easy to change. The point is to develop your capacity to leap *despite* the risk being outside your tolerance range and the prospect of fear being greater than you think you can handle. Hacking risk appetite so you take on the right level of risk, rather than the level that feels comfortable, is a bit like dieting. You have to commit irreversibly to a risk level before the actual fear kicks in, and then short-circuit the ability of your appetite to do anything about it.

It's like deciding to eat a salad for lunch and locking in that commitment by throwing away the cake and chips. Caesar burning bridges and Cortez burning boats are among many famous examples of leaders hacking risk appetite, but you have to go beyond resonating with such allegories to crafting literal irreversible commitment moves for yourself.

In my case, a big part of hacking my risk appetite was getting very small cash flows going. They were barely better than nothing in terms of actually sustaining my life financially, but they made a huge difference psychologically as proof that I could make money flow without help from an employer. Apparently my gut can't count and doesn't know the difference between $100 and $1000. I exploited that.

How do you know when you've hacked your risk appetite into submission? You've heard how entrepreneurs have to go from a logical *Ready, Aim, Fire* to an illogical *Ready, Fire, Aim* operating condition. Hacking risk appetite takes the illogic one step further. Your first leap is almost certainly going to be a case of *Fire, Aim, Ready.*

If you've hacked your risk appetite and worked on PROD as much as you can, it should feel like you're making the irreversible commitment *before* you've figured out a direction, and picked a direction and started moving *before* you're actually ready to sustain movement. It feels unnatural, but that's a good (if not dispositive) sign you're doing it right.

FIRE, AIM, READY

Okay, you've picked your leap date or event and it's N years out, or perhaps it's in the past: you've already leaped, underprepared. But no matter what N is for you, it's likely going to be a fire-aim-ready script. The question now is how much preparation can you cram into what time you have between *fire* and *ready* (which is possibly negative). Here's a rough breakdown, illustrated in the drawing.

$N<0$: You're in *preparation debt zone*. You've leaped and are not ready. Get active on Twitter. Create an interesting deck around a topic of expertise and see if you can line up talks at meetups and conferences (simply attending and "networking" is very low value). Make money by any means possible. Drive Lyft. Get a low-status temp job that seems beneath you if you must (but commit to quitting as soon as possible). Save money by any means possible, borrow if you must (and can). *N<0* is an emergency response regime and you will do most of this naturally because it is obvious. Your actions aren't going to be very leveraged or strategic. You're in band-aid territory. But getting out of the emergency mode will not necessarily happen naturally. It is surprisingly easy to adapt to, and stay in, this crappy temporizing zone far longer than you should. Your goal here is to start aggressively buying time so you can actually catch up on preparation work that should have been done before the leap. Preparation debt is not a good state to be in, and your survival chances are weakest, but it's not necessarily fatal. And it can be a better state to be in than in a soul-killing job.

0<N<1: You're in *launch ramp zone.* Count the number of friends outside your work you interact with regularly outside of work and increase that. They will be more valuable in the short term than shallow "networking" contacts or current at-work colleagues (who may feel betrayed and not inclined to help when you leave). Double or triple your investment in outside high-frequency friendships. If you're in a line of work that allows for creating outside-of-work artifacts, identify a small warm-up pre-gig like a *pro bono* project for a nonprofit or a contribution to an open-source project. And most importantly, *ramp up your performance at work.* Exiting on a high note creates a *lot* of positive externalities. And of course, start saving aggressively, on a war footing.

1<N<3: You're in *asset-building zone.* Between one and three years, you have enough time to build a meaningful asset like a blog, email newsletter, book, or side project from a cold start. Not only should you build an asset, you should have turned it on at a test level and had some validated success with it. Also: get on a steady savings ramp. Not in an illiquid form like a retirement account or a house, but in a form that can be rapidly liquidated. And these savings have to be above and beyond emergency savings (which for most employed people tends to be one to three months, so think in terms of six months out).

3<N<5: You're in *portfolio-building zone.* Between three and five years, you have enough time to build *more* than one asset. When I jumped ship, I had been developing the option for four years. Besides my main blog, Ribbonfarm, I had a book almost ready to go and a strong following on Quora. Try and cultivate *different* kinds of options that are not too correlated with each other. A book, once launched (especially if self-published), can instantly create a spike of revenue. In this planning range, your savings behavior still has to be slightly different (more loaded on liquid assets than people who intend to stay employed)

N>5: Beyond five years, we are in *mindset-preparedness zone.* The behaviors include: reading outside your sector, reading management and self-management books, and approaching your job with a very different mindset than the people who expect to stay in paycheck employment their whole careers. Preparing for the option of leaping into the gig economy might actually make you better at your job, ironically (it serves as a BATNA—best alternative to a negotiated agreement—that increases your risk-taking *at* your job, leading to better results since most employees take too little internal risk).

Training zone: If you're in college or high school, and the clock hasn't started ticking yet, you're in the *training zone.* If you're aware that the future is giggy, you will approach your educational options differently, and prioritize different skills than if you were preparing for a paycheck career in a series of jobs.

Contrarian view: if you're in education, I don't think it's a good idea to dive right into the gig economy. If you can, spend some time in a paycheck world first. Gigwork still uses all the same skills as paycheck work, so you might as well learn those skills on someone else's dime.

IN CONCLUSION

Here's the big boring secret about the gig economy. Though it is still a small fraction of the labor market (I'd estimate about 20–25% in the US, though economic statistics here are notoriously unreliable and tricky to interpret), *everybody* is likely to cycle through it at some point, at least for a while. There's nothing particularly special about being in the gig economy. The difference isn't between people who are/will be in it *vs.* not, but between people who are *happier* in it *vs.* not. Yet almost nobody prepares for it, intellectually, financially, emotionally, or educationally. Weird, huh?

Despite the fact that it will touch almost everybody's life in the future, it is somewhat magical: the gig economy exists only to the extent you believe in it. It is like an economic equivalent of the Room of Requirement in Harry Potter. You have to kinda believe it is out there and that it will appear around you when you need it.

The paycheck employment economy *also* only exists because we believe in it enough to jump into it, without guarantees that there's a place for us in it when we head out interviewing. The only difference is that the paycheck economy comes with a lot of highly visible social-proof props called "companies" that make belief easier, by building a concrete landscape of offices with reception desks, equipment, badges, and uniforms. Believing in the paycheck economy is like suspending disbelief enough to watch a movie. Believing in the gig economy is like suspending disbelief enough to read a book. You have to construct your own mental imagery to make it real.

A lot of economics is about self-fulfilling prophecies. Stuff that happens because people believe it can. When an economic sector dries up, all of it can turn into a ghost town overnight. Whether it is populated by gigworkers in cafes or employees with badges in offices makes no difference. The cafes empty out and close down. The offices empty out and close down. *For sale* signs go up. Tumbleweed blows in the wind. Zombies appear and stagger about.

Gigwork or paycheck work, we all live in the same economy. The only difference is how we manage our exposure to the risks of living inside the shared illusions of economic modernity.

To leap into the gig economy is to leap into a state of belief that does not require all the props. It is a state of belief that draws directly from the raw, collective *élan vital* of *homo economicus*, trusting in your fellow human beings to create the demand for whatever it is you might be capable of supplying. It is the opposite of flouncing out of the economy with a pile of fuck-you money. It is something like a trust fall into the waiting hands of unknown people who you are going to believe in, and who are going to believe in you, so you can invent your own future.

19

BOOTSTRAPPING WITH BEEFS
TO FIND CLIENTS, START BEEFS

THE MOST COMMON hard question I get around consulting work is: *how do I find clients to get bootstrapped as an indie consultant?* It is at once the most distastefully grubby practical question you can ask, and the most sublimely philosophical one.

In this chapter, I want to offer an answer based partly on a popular blog post of mine, The Internet of Beefs.[1] It's a genuinely dangerous answer that can screw up your indie consulting career if implemented poorly, so I want to present it with some care. Read the whole chapter through and think carefully before adopting this approach, since running with it half-assed can really blow up in your face and make you not just unretainable as a consultant, but too toxic to even employ in a regular job. This is not theoretical. I know people who've blown themselves up this way.

This is also my tribute chapter for Clayton Christensen, developer of the disruptive idea of disruption, who passed away the week before I wrote the newsletter version of this chapter. You could say that the answer I'm offering in this chapter is a way to approach indie consulting bootstrapping as a non-classical disruption problem. Non-classical because *you* are the disruptive product, not something you design.

Again, I am not being theatrical about the risks here. They are real. I offer some safety tips at the end. *Primum non nocere, caveat emptor,* etc.

BOOTSTRAPPING ≠ FIRST CLIENT

The question of getting clients is distastefully grubby because there are so many soul-destroying bad answers out there that will kinda-sorta work in the sense of generating income, but will dehumanize you and practically make you want to kill yourself. Which explains why so many of the people who seem able to make them work either clearly have no soul, or are in deep denial about their ongoing destruction of it.

On the other hand, it is sublimely philosophical because if you squint a bit, it is almost the same as *why do I exist and what is the meaning of* my *life?* Many aspiring indie consultants manage to land a first client via a mix of mighty struggling, selling themselves short, and luck. Then they fervently hope that that first gig will magically turn into a steady stream of gigs via referrals.

Then they are shocked when that doesn't happen. Landing the second client turns out to be just as hard or harder. And the third, and the fourth. Eventually beginner's luck dries up and they face gambler's ruin. Because that's what this approach is. Gambling. You aren't bootstrapping at all. You're just failing painfully slowly. Your best outcome is actually to fail fast enough that you can go back to the paycheck economy without your psyche destroyed by the experience. Bootstrapping is not about getting your first client, but discovering your first non-brute-force *mechanism* for driving demand that actually works.

Of the three layers of the free-agent world, discussed in *Ten Dimensions of Gigwork*, indie consultant, contractor, and platformer, the question is only meaningful and hard at the indie consultant level. The mechanism is simpler at lower levels of the gig economy. Contractors just have to do a slightly different version of a job hunt and platformers simply have to sign up on some website. They face what Peter Thiel called a *1-to-n* problem. You are solving for becoming the *n*th Photoshop jockey or the *n*th Uber driver.

Indie consultants are faced with a 0-1 challenge: true bootstrapping. You have to become the *first* version of yourself that there is a demand for. You have to arrive as a unique presence in a public economic space, not labor anonymously backstage. I don't have a general answer—this is very much a 1:1 coaching type problem—but I do have a general *approach* to an answer, which relies on beefs. Let me illustrate with my own case.

CASE STUDY: ME

Of the hundreds of articles I've written, the top three in terms of how much they drove cold inbound leads for consulting gigs are the following. What feature you think they have in common?

- *The Gervais Principle (2009):* A dark/satirical take on office politics and corporate sociopathy that went hugely viral back in the day.[2]
- *Entrepreneurs are the New Labor (2012):* A cynical take on heroic valorization of founders, arguing that VCs are to founders as management to labor.[3]
- *Fat Thinking and Economies of Variety (2016):* Argues for fat startups and messy, wasteful, play-like innovation over "lean" thinking.[4]

It's not that they are dark and satirical or contrarian. I've written other dark/satirical or contrarian things that led to no gigs. It's not that they showcase deep expertise in a subject. They don't. In fact they largely showcase my shallow, self-taught amateurishness on the underlying topics. It's not that they offer step-by-step playbooks to solving the problems they frame. They don't.

The correct answer is that they each pick a beef worth picking, but not too strongly. *The Gervais Principle* picked a beef against feel-good "nice" management thinking that dominated the pop-business literature at the time.[5] *Entrepreneurs are the New Labor* picked a beef against people in the tech sector shilling what has come to be known as "hustle porn" and flattering founders with a *hero* self-image that blinds them to industry dynamics and debilitating behaviors. *Fat Thinking* picked a beef with the lean six-sigma crowd in big corporations, and the lean startup crowd in the startup scene.

Importantly, none of these is what you might call "pure beef" where the fight and criticism of an opposed perspective are the main focus or content. They are what you might call "20% beef" where the starting point is rejecting some core sacred-cow axiom of a prevailing orthodoxy and then building something new and interesting on that foundation of principled dissent based on additional ideas and novel elements. It is something like rejecting Euclid's parallel line postulate and going out on a limb to see if you can build a non-Euclidean geometry.

For example, the assumptions I rejected in my three articles above are:

1. *Gervais Principle:* executives are nice and managers know what they're doing.
2. *New Labor:* entrepreneurs/founders are heroes.
3. *Fat Thinking:* efficiency and optimization are good things.

One good answer to how to bootstrap from 0 to 1 is: *indie consultants bootstrap with beefs.* It's not the only way, and it's certainly not the safest way, but it's a fun way that is very intellectually satisfying and validating when it works and is the opposite of soul-destroying and dehumanizing. But *implementing* that answer is a remarkably hard challenge because it involves a delicate bit of threading the needle, and sending a hard-to-fake disruption signal out in the world.

TOO MUCH BEEF, TOO LITTLE BEEF

Bootstrapping with beefs can fail in two ways: via too much beef or too little. On the one hand, you can adopt too beefy a posture and end up crashing into the Internet of Beefs.[6] This is pure downside.

I've done that. For example, an early book review I wrote, of *Blue Ocean Strategy* (2007), was pure beef. Another, a review of Seth Godin's *Tribes* (2008), had the same problem. In both cases, I stand by my criticism and believe they are bad books. But the point is, the reviews were 100% beef. I didn't reject selected premises and build something else better on an alternative foundation. In both cases, it would have been possible; I just didn't bother to do it. I did the equivalent of criticizing Euclid's *Elements* with a "geometry is bad and geometers are evil" line of attack rather than building a non-Euclidean geometry.

On the other hand, you can put in a lot of work into posts that solidly cover a topic in an entirely non-beefy way and get a lot of gratitude and praise, but generate no leads. This is a safe way to fail in the short term, but in the long term is death by slow starvation.

I've done that too. Three examples of my own are *The Seven Dimensions of Positioning*[7] in 2010, *Economies of Scale, Economies of Scope*[8] in 2012, and *Product-Driven vs. Customer-Driven*[9] in 2014. I had high hopes of all three as consulting lead-gen essays. Though I got a lot of praise and gratitude for them, *as lead-generation essays* they were utter flops. Why? Because they weren't alternatives to existing ways of doing things. They weren't non-Euclidean geometries. They weren't beefy disruptions of prevailing orthodoxies.

Bootstrapping with beefs doesn't have to be done with writing. You could do a book, or a talk, or a show-over-tell artifact that falsifies a commonly held belief via counterexample. Or even just a Twitter rant. If you're not a creator type, you could develop a sales pitch for use in 1:1 conversational selling that's based on a beefy take. There are many ways to go non-Euclidean.

Many ways, but no easy ways. Discovering and developing a

genuine beef into an artful calling card that lands you gigs is hard work. That's why it's a costly signal. You can't fake it with simple bullshitting. You have to put in the work of:

1. spotting a widespread pattern of disillusionment in the margins
2. identifying the prevailing orthodoxy driving the disillusionment
3. analyzing its foundations
4. rejecting one or more flawed premises fueling the disillusionment
5. adding imaginative alternative premises
6. running with it to see where the whole thing can take you
7. becoming *conscious* of *what* and *who* you're *for* and *against*
8. articulating it out there in public and *standing* behind it.

Yes, this is just Clayton Christensen's ideas applied to you, personally, as an idea economy product, finding and serving an underserved marginal market before attacking the core. The work is hard not because it takes effort or time. None of those articles took me more than a couple of days to write. *The work is hard because it takes a certain amount of courage and a good deal of taste.* If you don't feel a bit of an adrenalin rush, a sense of a fight-or-flight, a sense of burning bridges, while working on them, you're not doing it right. Without this work, you'll end up with either too much beef or too little beef and be left with either a pointless fight or deathly silence.

DIFFERENTIATION = RIGHT AMOUNT OF BEEF

Why does 20% beef work as a bootstrapping solution? In the previous section, I noted that indie consultants pursue a differentiation strategy in terms of Michael Porter's three generic strategies.[10] But most beginning indie consultants don't understand what differentiation *means* in our line of work. Even ones who've figured out a differentiation that works are often unsure about how or why it is working. They just pray it doesn't suddenly stop. Hell, I was that way as late as 2014, three years into my indie career, as evidenced by the date of the last of the failed lead-gen blog posts I mentioned in the previous section.

What is differentiation for an indie consultant? *Differentiation is the right amount of beef in your positioning; notionally about 20%.* Most mistakenly assume differentiation is about a nice website with pithy, superlative-laden positioning statements, glowing testimonials from nobodies, and professional headshots. All pulled together with a headline declaring something like "*I help executives deliver value by blah blah blah zzzzzz zzz.*"

No, that's not a differentiated offering. That's a commodity offering putting on a nice suit. See the thing is, as an indie consultant, you are *not* selling a product that can have different features relative to the competition. Nor are you claiming skills others lack or five-star ratings putting you in a top performance category. That's contractors and platformers, people who sell maker skills or just plain labor. *You are modeling a clear, generative way to break away from something that a lot of people are disillusioned with.*

You're offering an *irreversible* path of *political action.* You're making your support for that action *mean* something by association. You *are* meaning. Some of you will recognize the element of Hannah Arendt philosophy here: we're talking about *action* in a spotlight over *making* or *laboring* backstage. I recommend Arendt's *The Human Condition* as philosophical background reading here.

BEEFY POSITIONING

All indie consultant positioning that works amounts to: *it doesn't have to be this prevailing orthodox way that you've been disillusioned by, there is another, better way, and here's how you go down that road.* Even if there is a product-like element to what you're offering, like say a workshop or training package, it's not the quality or effectiveness that matters, but the fact that it embodies a true, bridges-burned alternative to something that isn't working. And when you're offering services to senior executives in particular, VP and up at mid-to-large companies, the "alternative way" is the sum total of what they're buying. They don't need your expertise. They are the experts in their business.

They don't need your hands-on doer skills. That's what contractors and employees are for, not consultants. They don't need raw labor. That's Uber-for-X, whatever their X is. They don't need you to deliver rah-rah motivation to drive the troops from mediocre to superlative performance. That's for middle managers and motivational speakers.

Executives typically got where they are *not* by being exceptional performers, but by being bold and opinionated decision-makers who took interesting risks with a broad but mediocre set of abilities. They're generally in the market for opinions worth betting on, not knowledge or skills *per se.*

They need you, as an ideological partner-in-arms, to drive an alternative-way agenda through. You are their ideological optionality. Betting on you should represent a meaningful risk. I learned this when one of my early clients literally introduced me to someone as his "secret weapon."

And you can't just create ideological optionality by painting a cloud of superlatives around your headshot and expect that halo of meaningless blather to do the work. You have to offer something like a weaponized schism that they can use to force a decision, and drive the action down one road rather than another. That's what the eight-step recipe I outlined earlier aims to craft. It's a tall order and fraught with all sorts of risks if you actually try it. So here are some safety rules for running this 20% beef bootstrapping playbook, whatever medium you choose.

SAFETY RULES!

Here's a set of twelve rules that can help to keep you safe and generative when you try to bootstrap with beefs (or level up your game). They aren't guaranteed to keep you perfectly safe. Conflict is by definition risky. You might misjudge a tone. You might push too hard or not hard enough. You might provoke someone who goes all psychopath on you. You might get hijacked by your own emotions and get sucked deeper into a fight than you intended. You might get distracted from trying to solve a real problem by the desire to make an adversary suffer. But still, following these rules should load things in your favor, and mitigate the risks.

1. Add three or four novel elements for every one rejected orthodoxy element.
2. Use the Warren Buffett rule: praise by name, criticize by category.
3. Offer an exit to a better way, rather than a voice in a fight.
4. Bring out the funny side, which is not the same as being haha funny.
5. Reject what you reject with force and clarity, don't pull your punches.
6. Embrace what you embrace with doubt and qualifications.
7. Follow your truth where it leads you, not your adversaries where they draw you.
8. Openly acknowledge any motivating resentments *and set them aside.*
9. You don't have to pick every battle, *but you do have to pick a few.*
10. Disengage from the rejected way, do not seek to destroy it.

11. Firmly reject resentment-driven supporters who want to fight for you.
12. Be kind. If you forget every other rule, don't forget this one.

That's it. Go forth and disrupt, with 20% beef.

---

1. www.ribbonfarm.com/2020/01/16/the-internet-of-beefs/
2. www.ribbonfarm.com/2009/10/07/the-gervais-principle-or-the-office-according-to-the-office/
3. www.forbes.com/sites/venkateshrao/2012/09/03/entrepreneurs-are-the-new-labor-part-i/#7f9fea7f4eab
4. www.ribbonfarm.com/2016/07/28/fat-thinking-and-economies-of-variety/
5. I helped drive the surge of interest in darker understandings of business circa 2009–12 I think.
6. www.ribbonfarm.com/2020/01/16/the-internet-of-beefs/
7. www.ribbonfarm.com/2010/09/21/the-seven-dimensions-of-positioning/
8. www.ribbonfarm.com/2012/10/15/economies-of-scale-economies-of-scope/
9. www.ribbonfarm.com/2014/04/24/product-driven-versus-customer-driven/
10. Differentiation is indie consultants, focus is contractors, low-cost leadership is platformers.

SECTION FOUR

MANAGING
PERCEPTIONS

In this world which we enter, appearing from a nowhere, and from which we disappear into a nowhere, *Being and Appearing coincide*... Nothing and nobody exists in this world whose very being does not presuppose a *spectator*.

HANNAH ARENDT

20

WHEN IS A GIG AN ENGAGEMENT?

THE IMPORTANCE OF NOT HAGGLING

I RECENTLY READ a line in Terry Pratchett's *Hogfather* that made me laugh out loud because it precisely nails the important intrinsic difference between consultants and contractors.[1] The situation is that a high-profile member of the Guild of Assassins is talking to a bunch of contract-muscle types for a job, and one of the contractors uses the word *employed* to refer to the team's relationship to the client.

> He bridled at this. Assassins were never employed. They were engaged or retained or commissioned, but never *employed*. Only servants were employed.

As an indie *consultant*, you too are always engaged, never employed. A mark of this is that you almost never haggle over your price. It doesn't matter what title you give yourself, what expertise you offer, or how much you charge. If you end up haggling, you're a contractor, not a consultant. You're employed, not engaged.

This is a social distinction, not a financial one, and it matters because it sets the tone of your working life. Many contractors make way more money than consultants, and might bill at much higher rates. But an \$800/hour gigworker who gets bargained down to \$600 in an explicit negotiation, with talk of guaranteed hours and such, is a contractor. A \$150/hour gigworker who always gets either a yes or no, but no haggling counter-offers, is likely a true consultant (non-haggling is necessary but not sufficient).

What difference does this distinction make? A big one. Consultants have quasi-social relationships with clients, with nonfinancial aspects you may or may not value. In fact there are three zones here:

1. *Transactional:* you haggle, but you don't expect more than civil social interactions around the gig. Chatting outside the scope of the transactional relationship will feel like inappropriate voyeuristic curiosity about a different social milieu to both sides.
2. *Quasi-social:* you don't haggle, and you become at least casual friends who enjoy chatting outside the scope of the engagement around shared interests that are socially native for both of you in your respective milieus. You probably participate in the occasional unbilled social interaction like a dinner party, where you don't talk shop. But you probably don't get angry or fight.
3. *Intimate:* the relationship is close enough for yelling and screaming and talking about money the way families do internally. Money matters are on the table and up for discussion, but not in the same way as they are when haggling with a vendor in a marketplace. Disagreement is unlikely to end in walking away from each other.[2]

If you've successfully positioned yourself as a consultant, you're in the quasi-social zone and people will either say yes or no to the price you quote. If nobody ever says no, you've priced your services too low.

Or they'll judge your sense of your own worth accurately them-selves and make you an offer that works for you, and *you* can simply say yes. If anyone makes an offer that simply feels insulting to you, you've either overestimated your worth or badly miscom-municated your capabilities. People rarely knowingly lowball you unless they are assholes *and* know you are under some kind of pressure that might lead you to give them a bargain deal. If on the other hand their offer is shockingly higher than you expect, some-thing weird is going on that you should figure out. Check that you're not accidentally working for the mob, as happened to Tom Cruise in *The Firm.*

You still have to occasionally recalibrate and reset your price as you gain experience and build a track record, and the occasional larger-scope anchor gig will need more custom pricing design. But in general, as a consultant, you don't haggle in individual trans-actions.

Why this dynamic? Because consulting is an intellectual part-nership that is too bespoke to easily compare to substitutes, and only works if both parties see each other as fully human. The rela-tionship is a bit above pricing discussions. If a client sees you as a functional and sharply scope-limited cog producing a deliverable component of a larger activity, that's a contracting relationship.

In consulting, all parties are contributing to the outcome in highly entangled ways that make it hard to break out and accu-rately value a given individual's contribution. In contracting, the contractor typically has clear measures for their own success or failure, independent of the overall success or failure of a project, and a way to value their piece of the puzzle.

When a client truly sees you as a consultant, the choice they are making is not between you and someone else similar to you. Their choice is between doing it one way with you in the picture and doing it a different way without you. It's like a marriage: the client is choosing between different *lives,* not between interchangeable people who might fit into the same slot in a life template that doesn't change. The old joke about a man hiring a prostitute gets at this tension from the other side.

Man: Will you sleep with me for $1 million?

Woman: Okay

Man: Will you sleep with me for $5?

Woman: *What!* What kind of woman do you take me for?

Man: We've already established what kind of woman you are. Now we're just haggling over the price.

If you're interested in a more general understanding of the socioeconomic dynamics at work here, read my old blog posts *The Economics of Pricelessness*[3] and *Bargaining With Your Right Brain.*[4] Approach pricing your services as a consultant the way you approach making a restaurant suggestion if someone offers to buy you dinner. You will make a suggestion that is acceptable to both of you socially, because the main point is to spend time together, not maximize the dollar or caloric value of the food you can get out of it. If you can't think of a restaurant where you can both feel comfortable, and able to focus on each other's company rather than the dining experience, you're not going to be socializing at all.

Think of how awkward a restaurant outing would be if you suggested a super-pricey place you would never pay to go to yourself, and ordered the most expensive things possible, like it's your one chance to be in that environment. Or if you suggested an all-you-can-eat buffet and gorged yourself like you hadn't eaten in a week.

Neither is conducive to actually having a fruitful relationship with the person paying. In one case your host would be giving you a tour of a social class out of your reach, while graciously ignoring your gaucherie; in the other case they'd be feeding you because you're starving and only pretending to keep you company socially.

Do not assume though, that simply because there is no haggling, the price agreed upon is irrational or somehow divorced from demand-and-supply dynamics. Generally what's going on, when a gig lands in the consulting zone, is that the value in play is so high that whatever the consultant is being paid is almost a rounding error relative to the value of a potentially successful outcome.

In most gigs I've taken on, I'd estimate that my billings represent less than 0.5% of the economic value in play. Usually much less, in the case of large companies navigating really big decisions and problems. That doesn't mean I'm personally on the hook for delivering 0.5% of the value. Things are generally too entangled to make such determinations. All it means is that my *cost fraction* is low enough that it's not worth optimizing. For cost management, there are bigger levers available to work with than nickel-and-diming me.

Or for personal gigs with a life-coaching or therapeutic tone, the value in play is their health, happiness, or sanity, all of which are generally priceless to anyone, no matter how rich. Which means if they can pay at all, they're not going to argue about the price. They're not in that headspace (which means it is even more crucial for *you* to be careful not to exploit that trust).

Make sure you actually *want* such ambiguous quasi-social relationships around high-stakes personal or organizational activities, by the way, and are not just defaulting into this mode in trying to avoid the awkwardness of bargaining where bargaining is in fact both possible and called for.

If so, it may be better to position yourself as a contractor, and develop a structured bargaining approach if it fits your goals better. It's one thing to recognize and adapt to the social narrative surrounding a gig, quite another to become attached to it at the cost of your financial health. If you are avoiding negotiating simply because you find it demeaning or stressful, you're doing it wrong.

But if you do like the quasi-social nature of consulting, and you successfully position yourself as a consultant, then price yourself right for it to be a sustainable lifestyle, and try to get to yes/no via 1-step negotiations, with pricing resets every year or two.

------

1. The Discworld novels are excellent reading for consultants of all types by the way.
2. Truly intimate relationships are rare in gigwork, though mildly intimate ones are common.
3. www.ribbonfarm.com/2014/08/12/the-economics-of-pricelessness/
4. www.ribbonfarm.com/2008/03/16/bargaining-with-your-right-brain/

21

A SELF-IMAGE IS A DANGEROUS THING

BEWARE IDENTITY ATTACHMENTS

WHAT SHOULD your self-image as an indie consultant be? Take a moment to pick an option before reading further:

- martial artist
- pattern-language maven
- storyteller/bard
- no-bullshit grinder

There are others, but these are the most common self-images I see in people entering the indie consulting game. Each self-image induces a certain kind of structure to replace the structure you're leaving behind. Which is the right answer?

PAYCHECKIER THAN THOU

This is a trick question, and all these answers are wrong. There *is* a right answer, but first let me explain why your answer is wrong. Your answer is wrong because each answer is basically an ersatz version of a salaried consultant: a paycheck employee of an established, brand-name, industrial-era consulting firm.

If that's all indie consulting is—offering ersatz versions of services offered by consulting firms, for less money, and at smaller scale—then it is basically not worth doing. You may make money, but you likely won't be fulfilled. You'll always feel like a second-class citizen in a game pioneered by others that they're better at. A cheaper knock-off of a major brand.

There is a place in the consulting economy for the things salaried consultants do, and for the brand-name consulting firms that employ them, but it's not your place. It's not your game.

So why do we gravitate to these self-images? Because uncritical imitation is easier than thinking about your own situation. That, plus easy availability of real people to imitate. And the fact that they are familiar images to project to clients, making for easy (if not particularly effective) marketing and sales strategies.

The last few decades, from the 1970s to the early 2000s, were something of an aberration in the history of consulting, in that the craft became highly stylized, corporatized, and dominated by the *non*-independent kind of consultant. Consultants who were employees of larger consulting companies, which aggregated talent capable of delivering against a particular consulting playbook.

Not only are typical consultants paycheck types, they are more paychecky than ordinary paycheck types, not less. Despite a superficial mercenary branding, rank-and-file employee consultants are the truest Organization Men, taking on *less* career risk in general than employees, not more. Consulting from within a large, established consulting firm is often a *safer* line of work than regular paycheck jobs, not riskier. If you get laid off from a consulting-firm job, you have more options open to you, in more industries, than a regular laid-off employee.

Cynicism about flavor-of-the-month business fads is for client employees. Salaried consultants are usually true believers not only in whatever kool-aid they sell, but in the general idea of the industrial corporation as a model for organizing work. They are Extreme Organization Men (and Women). Upton Sinclair once observed, "It is difficult to get a man to understand something when his salary depends upon his not understanding it." When your salary depends upon not understanding that you're selling kool-aid, you will work hard to not understand it.

The ordinary paycheck employee merely suffers through the latest flavor of the month, finding solace in watercooler grousing and *Dilbert* comic strips. The sociopath CEOs and the partner-level consultants selling them services merely practice the age-old art of collaborative cronyist ruling from the top.

But the rank-and-file consultants actually delivering the goods? Goods ranging from agile software workshops and design thinking to brand-narrative studies and heavy-lift spreadsheet models? They believe. They have to. Their livelihoods depend on it. What's more, not only do they believe, they think they are part of a more enlightened breed, tasked with raising the consciousness of cynical and apathetic regular employees with their wisdom. They think their kool-aid is red pills.

Red pills for a particular subset of traditional employees.

Each of the four self-images in the opening poll represents an archetype that is symbiotic with a class of roles within traditional organizations. There are four such classes, giving us four True Believer paycheckier-than-thou salaried consultant types.

TRUE BELIEVER SALARIED CONSULTANTS

The industrial-age corporation comprises four types of employees, each served by its salaried consultant symbiote type:

- rank-and-file workers, served by *martial-artist trainer* types
- staff management, served by *pattern-language maven* types
- executive leadership, served by *storyteller/bard* types
- line management, served by *no-bullshit grinder* types

Notably, very little of the actual playbook-deliverable work is done by senior partners in consulting firms, who do take on non-employee type risks. Let's take these four types in turn. Don't forget: these are *salaried* consulting archetypes. They are paycheck-ier-than-thou Extreme Organization Men.

The *martial-artist trainer* self-image was pioneered by produc-tivity/efficiency focused consulting companies that offered training programs for skilled rank-and-file employees. Things like lean six-sigma, agile programming, and so forth. Programmers seeking philosophical inspiration often naturally turn to Asian martial arts because they feed a nerdy OCD approach to personal growth. They try to map martial arts concepts like *shuhari* and *kihon-kata-kumite* to the problem of becoming more technically proficient. Consulting firms operating in this market gleefully co-opt this tendency in offerings like lean six-sigma with its "belt" system, or "coding katas" used by agile programming trainers. *Participation in such offerings feels like fandom to clients.*

The *pattern-language maven* self-image was pioneered by design consulting firms, many drawing inspiration from the work of architectural thinkers like Christopher Alexander, that pandered to the vanities of aesthetes and wannabe autocrats seeking compre-hensive "systems" for running little empires. Often, the target kind of client for such firms is people in staff roles without too much direct power over P&Ls. Such people are often in denial about their lack of real agency relative to line management, and eagerly latch on to any "system" that allows them to produce and consume process make-work with combinatorial efficiency. A dead give-away is the production of stylized information artifacts for their own sake. *Participation in such offerings feels like cultural/art produc-tion to clients.*

The *storyteller/bard* self-image was pioneered by marketing and advertising firms in the era when powerful advertising firms led by charismatic ad-men managed powerful brands and huge broadcast media budgets, farming out vast cascades of work in everything from graphic design to video production. The target was often vain senior executives in a mood to buy self-serving narratives which would offer them starring roles and a delusion of more authorship over events than they actually had, while helping manage the optics of whatever universe-denting they were pretending to do. Often this kind of aspirational self-deception evolves in parallel with cynical stock manipulation to maximize financial payoffs. *Participation in such offerings feels like history-making or theatrical production of quasi-historical narrative—often both at once—to clients.*

The *no-bullshit grinder* self-image is the most familiar of the four and was pioneered by the Big-Three strategy consulting firms who made the archetypal modern consultant a familiar figure: putting in 100-hour weeks, logging hundreds of thousands of frequent flyer miles, living out of hotels and weekend apartments. The calling card of this breed was the wonky spreadsheet, with which they "got real," typically with the P & L line management types. *Participation in such offerings often feels like martyred "real" work to clients.* What is common to all four breeds is that they are paycheck employees who:

1. log billable hours but are protected from revenue volatility
2. often work far harder than employees at the companies they serve
3. are true believers in whatever playbook they're running
4. believe they're enlightened cynics who see reality more clearly than clients
5. believe more strongly in the roles they serve than the people occupying them
6. aestheticize an area of work in ways that flatter the self-images of clients

This is why I call them paycheckier-than-thou. All four are terrible archetypes to model your indie consulting career on.

THE RIGHT ANSWER

I don't want to be too hard on these archetypes. The playbooks they run offer a *lot* of good raw material for indie consultants. You can, and should, liberally steal from, and adapt, all four kinds of True Believer paycheckier-than-thou playbooks. You should mix-and-match gleefully. You should use their techniques the way guerrillas use the weapons they steal from the larger conventional armies they go up against. I do this liberally, stealing from all four sources all the time.

But what you *shouldn't* do is adopt the associated self-images or overarching playbooks.

As an indie consultant, your situation is opposite that of salaried consultants. Your livelihood depends on understanding what the traditional consulting industry, in the form of larger firms, actually does. That's the only way you'll find a guerrilla niche for yourself in the landscape they've carved out. salaried consultant self-images are liabilities for independent consulting. Your logged hours represent real money. Your attachment to every client rests entirely on the value of the last valuable thing you did for them. You cannot hide within the nebulous value proposition of a million-dollar engagement between two corporations. Your contributions (or lack thereof) cannot be safely hidden within the work of a large team.

For the salaried consultant, there is no difference between running a playbook and making a difference. For the indie consultant, there is all the difference in the world. Believing in any kind of kool-aid is an existential risk for you, even though it is a crucial enabler for some breed of salaried consultant.

- To the extent indie consulting is like martial arts training, it is closer to supporting someone as a wingman in a street fight than coaching them in a stylized dojo. You're not Yoda, you're Han Solo.

- To the extent indie consulting is a pattern language, it is a jury-rigged library of cheap tricks collected from all over the place rather than a systematic aesthetic theory. You're not Christopher Alexander, you're a dumpster diver.
- To the extent indie consulting is about storytelling, it is a shredded pile of narrative fragments, lending structure to moments of clarity in chaos rather than producing epics. You're not Walter Isaacson, you're a stand-up comic.
- To the extent indie consulting is about no-bullshit grinding, it is about finding and doing the few hours of work that actually matter, buried in the 100-hour makework-week. You're not Ray Donovan, but neither are you Tim Ferris, solving for four work hours. You're a mystery-solving detective, putting in the hours needed to solve the case correctly. Sometimes that's a 100-hour work week, sometimes it's a 4-hour work week, and it's never a straight line from interviews to spreadsheets to powerpoints.

When you put these fragmentary aspects together, you get only one answer: the indie consultant is a trickster, cobbling together bits and pieces of identities in an ongoing improvisation, sometimes sublime and inspired, sometimes just buying you enough time to dream up the next hack. The indie-consultant life is an endless Halloween, a string of trick-or-treat encounters with clients who generously play along, where the only thing keeping you philosophically honest is the fact that you have to live with yourself, with no playbooks or Senior Partners to blame for your failures.

And the goal of the trickery is to fool yourself *and* the client just long enough to accidentally do something right. And if you're lucky, maybe some of the tricks will be treats too.

22

SNEAKING AWAY FROM YOURSELF

YOU'RE A BAD BOSS AND YOU SHOULD SNEAK AWAY FROM YOURSELF

THERE'S a gig-economy disease that will likely strike you within a couple of years of going indie, if you succeed by sticking the landing in your first leap. You'll find that you have periods with plenty of nominally free time, but mysteriously, no time for the kinds of passion projects, such as writing, independent research, maker projects, or travel, that probably motivated you to quit in the first place. I'll call this disease *sneakoffproofitis*.

| Sneaking away from yourself

The problem is, as a free agent, you are your own boss, and you're likely a bad boss, unable to relax, and driven by fretful anxiety about lining up the next gig. That would be bad enough, except that you're also an *omniscient* bad boss. You know all your own tricks and nothing is hidden from you. You can't sneak away from yourself. You have sneakoffproofitis.

Here's what sneakoffproofitis looks like. Your bank balance looks healthy for the moment. You have enough work lined up so the cash flow looks good for the next few months. You've only committed a modest fraction of your hours—say ten a week—to deliver that work. You're temporarily cash rich *and* time rich. It's a sweet situation, right? So why is it so hard to take your time/money surplus and do something interesting with it?

The thing is, *fun things are only fun when you sneak off from things that feel like work to do them.* There is a certain creative freedom that is unleashed when you're using up free time that feels like it is stolen from commitments towards necessary work. The courage demanded by the time theft fuels boldness in the sneak-off activity. This is funny because the idea of time theft is only well-defined for robotic labor where you are paid to execute a production algorithm, with a clear relationship between time and output. It is incoherent when applied to knowledge work where there is only a weak correlation between time spent at work and the quality/quantity of output.

But our sneak-off instincts are still linked to robotic labor modes of production. Time isn't high-quality creative time unless it feels a little bit stolen (which is why, paradoxically, fuck-you money can be a creativity killer).

The work of the knowledge worker is never done. You can always do an infinite amount of work for a finite piece of output. There are always more plans you could make, more background research you could do, more skills you could develop, more trends you could stay updated on, more refinements you could add to the slide deck, more Q&A you could prepare for. Knowledge work is something like insurance, and it can always be made to violate the law of diminishing marginal returns if you're neurotic enough to keep buying.

This is as true of the free-agent life as it is of the paycheck life. There are always more lead-generating blog posts you could write, more pitches you could send out, more tweaks you could make to your website, more spec-work you could do to go gig-fishing with, more RFPs you could respond to, more clever tweets you could put out to draw viral attention.

And the bad-omniscient-boss side of you knows this. And won't let the sneak-off-to-play side of you sneak off to do anything else while there are productive things you could be doing. That's sneakoffproofitis.

What's the cure? Well, you could get brain surgery to separate the omniscient-bad-boss you from the sneak-off-to-play you, and have the latter hide stuff from the former (weirdly, things like this do happen with brain-damaged patients), but there's an easier way. You ratchet up the boldness of playful-you and sneak off *despite* the fact that the omniscient bad-boss is yelling at you.

Because here's the secret: omniscient-bad-boss-you is all-knowing and all-seeing, but *not* all-powerful. Omniscience does not imply omnipotence. In fact, omniscient-bad-boss-you is quite impotent compared to your old other-person boss. What are they going to do? Fire you?

You still need a principle to manage your sneaking-off though, and a way to balance sneak-off behaviors against money-making behaviors.

The principle I suggest is this: *pay yourself first*. You have probably heard that line from financial advisors. The idea is to put money in retirement savings accounts first, before spending money on other things. It's that idea, except with time, and with sneak-off activities rather than a retirement account being the target.

So when you have some freedom in how to allocate time towards necessary commitments (for example you have five hours of work due to a client, but the deadline is a week off and a to-do item to update your website before a speaking gig two weeks away) *vs.* sneak-off activities, *sneak-off and have fun first.*

Subtle point: you have to fill up all available time with necessary activities before you can actually sneak off. So if you typically plan in terms of a forty-hour week, on Monday morning, make a to-do list of "necessary" things that "must" get done "asap" and will take forty hours. For safety, overcommit and put sixty hours worth of work on the list. Then sneak off.

Before attacking that list.

Sneaking off from an under-full to-do list doesn't work, just as weight-training with no weights doesn't work. You strengthen your sneak-off boldness by stealing from *committed* time, not by clearing and occupying free time. That's just a hobby bad-boss-you tolerates.

Sneaking off is how you reveal your own sense of priorities and urgencies to yourself. You don't know whether or not something can wait unless you try to sneak off from doing it. And unlike carved-out free time, sneak-off time has no preset boundaries. How long you stay in sneak-off mode is determined by the tug o' war between your to-do anxiety and the strength of your absorption in the sneak-off activity.

Yes, your omniscient bad-boss side will scream and bully, but you can ignore that. Learning to ignore your own screaming and bullying is the whole point of sneak-off behaviors. Quitting a paycheck job and earning your freedom from others is the easy part. You aren't truly free until you've earned freedom from your *own* ridiculous expectations of yourself.

The logic of paying yourself first is similar to retirement savings prioritization logic. The things you do in your sneak-off time are the things that have a chance of turning into long-term compounding assets. But watch out for a related disease, *projectitis*: omniscient-bad-boss you will attempt to turn every such activity into a legible project at the first whiff of a possible return, and ruin both the fun and the possibility. Eventually you have to let that happen if the activity grows enough, but delay the onset of projectitis, and stay in sneak-off-and-play mode, as long as possible.

In the short term sneak-off activities are bugs in your self-imposed productivity regimen, but in the long term, they're the main feature of the lifestyle you're constructing and the *most* necessary among all the things you must do.

Neglect sneak-off activities at your own peril. All work and no play make Jack a dull paycheck employee, but a dead free agent.

23

YOU ARE NOT A PARASITE

WEAK ORGANIZATIONS ALWAYS HARBOR PARASITES. ARE YOU ONE?

IT'S newbie-consultant vaccination time (and booster-shot week for the experienced ones who may have learned and forgotten the lesson I want to talk about). The vaccine comes in the form of this triangle, and is meant to protect you from an operational hazard of indie consulting: charges of parasitism.

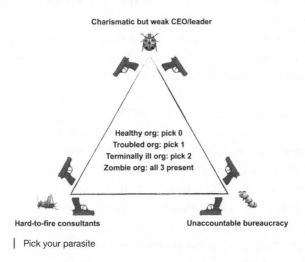

Charismatic but weak CEO/leader

Healthy org: pick 0
Troubled org: pick 1
Terminally ill org: pick 2
Zombie org: all 3 present

Hard-to-fire consultants   Unaccountable bureaucracy

| Pick your parasite

More specifically, the vaccine is meant to protect your psyche against the constant gaslighting and broad-strokes scapegoating of consultants by other kinds of economic actors, making you doubt your own economic worth relative to theirs, and wonder whether perhaps you *are* in fact morally inferior to them, as they insidiously keep suggesting, with their holier-than-thou sermonizing.

PARASITIC COMPETITION

The gaslighting and scapegoating of consultants is most likely to be led by two species of parasites that compete with parasitic consultants (who do exist) to feed on weak organizations: *charismatic but weak leaders*, and *unaccountable bureaucrats*.

To vaccinate yourself, you must learn to identify and counter the trash-talk from these two wonders of organizational ecosystems. You must learn to firmly defend your worth, especially to yourself. And even go on the offensive in internal battles if necessary, if you believe you are being unfairly maligned as a parasite, when you are in fact a Good Gigster fighting the Good Fight against the *actual* parasites. Here's the basic dynamic you have to understand.

As organizations weaken, all three species in their non-parasitic forms become subject to the morally hazardous incentives that lead to parasitic behaviors. Usually two of the species will appear together, and act to lock out the third, making it a two-way duel. And sometimes, only one of these species will appear, and cut off the other two. But in seriously weakened organizations, all three are often present, leading to a three-way standoff among them, with shifting alliances as the situation unfolds. This is the situation I've illustrated above in the cartoon (the locust, ladybug, and caterpillar in the diagram above are pests rather than parasites, but oh well, you get the point).

Consultants, as outsiders with no *locus standi* in the official narrative, and biased towards public silence by both long term business-model considerations and contractual obligations, are naturally vulnerable to being blamed for the effects of parasitism, *whether or not they are actually the parasites in a particular case.*

Basically, because you don't want to gain a reputation for throwing your clients under the bus under stress, and because non-disclosure and non-disparagement clauses probably make it legally risky to do so anyway, you are easy and safe to blame. Perversely, this can make angry consultants, who feel unfairly maligned, *turn* parasitic even if they weren't previously. The tempting line of reasoning goes: might as well be hanged for a sheep as a lamb, and get yours while the getting is good.

Charismatic and weak leaders and unaccountable bureaucrats aren't the only ones who like to preach anti-consultant sermons, and score cheap points by tarring our noble trade with a broad brush. But they are the ones who matter, because they are in a position to affect the roles consultants might be playing, and also know enough to be *effectively* disingenuous in their anti-consultant sermonizing.

Others who join in, especially in the media, tend to have no idea what they're talking about. Their unaided criticism (sincere or disingenuous) tends to be so wide off the mark, it does little to no damage. But competing parasites can sometimes co-opt these less effective critics and target their outrage to be more effective.

Assuming you're among the good players who aren't actually being parasitic in their gigwork, vulnerability to undeserved charges of parasitism creates two problems for indie consultants in particular. The easier problem is making yourself *practically* immune to accusations of parasitism and structurally distancing yourself from actually parasitic consultants. The harder problem, and the one the triangle vaccine is meant to address, is hardening your psyche against the gaslighting, making you *philosophically* immune to it.

Let's tackle the harder problem first, because it will make the easy problem even easier.

PHILOSOPHICAL IMMUNIZATION

The key to philosophical immunity is to firmly call bullshit on the holier-than-thou moral posturing that usually lies behind accusations of consultant parasitism. The key to this is understanding *who* feels threatened by the presence of consultants (whether honest or actually parasitic), when, and why.

Organizations are vulnerable to *three* kinds of parasites when they are in poor health.

1. *Charismatic but weak CEOs/leaders* who function by creating strong reality distortion fields around gaps in their weak leadership. They are vulnerable to their reality distortion fields being punctured by skeptical, informed scrutiny.

2. *Unaccountable bureaucracies* that quietly control the organization from the inside and are vulnerable to their internal monitoring and inspection processes being revealed as ceremonial shams protecting inefficiency, ineffectiveness, incompetence, or profiteering by skeptical, informed scrutiny. Think lifers at government agencies. Or most old-economy big companies.

3. *Hard-to-fire consultants* who get their hooks into organizations, and make themselves indispensable to the day-to-day functioning once they are in. They are vulnerable to their work being exposed as self-serving and against the interests of the organization by skeptical, informed scrutiny. Think the worst kinds of Big-Three engagements.

For each of these bad-actor species, the other two kinds of bad actors represent competition in the feeding frenzy, but the bigger threat is *good-actor* types at the other two vertices because they are the ones who can direct the skeptical informed scrutiny at them, and lead efforts to resist and reverse the parasitized organizational condition:

1. Strong, effective CEOs who don't need to distort reality to cover up weaknesses in order to either lead the organization or profit personally.
2. Professional, high-integrity bureaucracies whose processes can pass internal or external scrutiny with flying colors.
3. Good consultants who can cast an unflattering light on internal realities and self-congratulatory narratives through pointed, detailed, and specific external comparisons.

Notably, Steve Jobs distorted reality primarily to create missionary motivation at Apple rather than cover up his own weaknesses, and equally notably, his is among the rare criticisms of consultants that are fair,[1] based on the breadth-over-depth tradeoff we consultants must make, rather than glib charges of default-parasitic tendencies (his opening line in the interview cited above: "I don't think there is anything inherently evil in consulting").

The key to immunizing yourself is to tag the primary source of the accusations in a given case, reject their default claim to the moral high ground (and default insidious suggestion that the consultant must necessarily be the parasite, kinda like the Butler Did It default), and uncover the actual pattern of parasitism going on. Which might lead on to . . .

FIGHTING THE GOOD FIGHT

Once you've uncovered it to your satisfaction, the actual pattern of parasitism in a weak organization is not necessarily information you need to act on. The organization may be naturally defending itself, and you may be able to add value without getting involved.

You just need to become aware of it to protect your psyche against gaslighting, and dodge scapegoating attempts.

But if need be—and such need indicates the gig has turned into a war zone at a seriously weakened organization—you can choose to direct skeptical scrutiny where you think something is *actually* going on. What weakness or fraud is a charismatic but weak leader hiding? What processes are career bureaucrats protecting from skeptical inspection? These questions are weapons with which you can go on the offensive if you feel things are going beyond generic knee-jerk gaslighting of consultants, and you're actively being set up for unfair blame.

That is, of course, if it is worth your while to stay and fight at all, not just at a personal level, but at the level of your sense that the organization has value to the world, is worth curing of its parasitic infestations, and that you can be a meaningful part of the cure. Philosophical immunity is necessary if you want to survive as a consultant, because it is very rare for consultants to be engaged to help completely healthy organizations, and very easy to buy into hostile "parasite" perceptions of yourself. Chances are, there is a little bit of parasitic infection of all three kinds.[2]

INTERNAL ALLIES

Not every gig is a standoff of three-way competitive parasitism, and you don't have to stay and fight in all of the ones that are. But chances are you won't have the luxury of always working for healthy organizations. Some fraction of your gigs will involve parasite-fights, and of those, you'll have to pick a few to actually get into, because they are Good Fights.

If you walk away from all of them, not only will you forgo a big slice of the consulting pie, you will fail to grow in courage and integrity as a consultant. So you must pick a few fights. Every gig need not be an anti-parasite fight, but a few should be. Still, it's hard to fight the good fight to save an organization when nobody within it seems to want to. This means, it's only worth fighting when you have effective and sufficiently powerful internal allies who are fighting for what's worth saving.

Assuming you've philosophically immunized yourself against charges of parasitism, the three most common allies who make for a fight worth fighting in an unhealthy organization are:

1. an effective CEO/leader against an unaccountable bureaucracy
2. a effective and competent bureaucracy against an unprincipled predatory weak charismatic CEO/leader trying to feed on the organization
3. an effective senior leader who is not the top leader/CEO but has enough personal credibility and sophistication to lead a reform campaign despite the presence of an unaccountable bureaucracy and/or a weak and charismatic CEO

That third pattern is surprisingly common. One of the tells of a weak but charismatic CEO is that they tend to allow high-level exceptions in their reality distortion field to make room for competent subordinates they cannot do without. While their *general* leadership posture is demanding unquestioned loyalty from their inner circle, and cult-like reverence from employees and customers who don't see them close-up, they tend to compromise that posture where they must.

A good principle to remember this pattern is John Boyd's advice: if your boss demands loyalty, give him integrity, if he demands integrity, give him loyalty. Let's call a senior leader who plays by this rule a Boydian Lieutenant. A holy warrior willing to lead the Good Fight internally. These make great allies and clients.

Extremely weak leaders, or ones preparing to exit with their loot (possibly killing the organization in the process), tend to demand loyalty and accept nothing but loyalty. But the ones with better survival instincts tend to make exceptions for indispensable Boydian Lieutenants. They are the only ones excused from having to pretend to believe in the reality-distortion field. They are the only ones excused from frequent and fervent inner-circle displays of loyalty towards the Dear Leader. They are the ones equipped to lead a Good Fight.

In summary: philosophical immunization against charges of parasitism amounts to recognizing the pattern of competitive parasitism that infects weakening organizations, correctly redirecting unfair charges and gaslighting to the guilty competing parasites and being prepared to go on the offensive and bring skeptical scrutiny to their behaviors when you feel the fight is a Good Fight. If you have that mindset, the practical immunization is easy.

PRACTICAL IMMUNIZATION

Once you have the mental models for philosophical immunization in place, are able to deflect routine gaslighting, and are armed with the information to go on the offensive if necessary, you are actually equipped to do some good in your gigs.

But there's a matter of practical immunization. It is not enough to have the philosophically hardened mindset. You must structure gigs tactically for defensibility against false charges, insinuations, or perceptions of parasitism.

Here's the key trick: make yourself *hard to hire, hard to retain*, and *easy to fire*. (*Hard to retain* as in hard to keep you paid, benched, and available without actually giving you things to do). Most consultants and consulting firms do the exact opposite. They strive to be easy to hire and retain, and hard to fire.

Worse, they do all they can to structure gigs with hooks for passive income, unnecessary maintenance work done on autopilot, and front-loaded non-optional work as a precondition for working with a client. That last item is a particularly clear tell of a potentially parasitic consultant.

Example: a publicist firm I once worked with on a project many moons ago insisted on front-loading a $7,500 item into the contract (we negotiated it down to $2,500 and a cross-promotional barter clause) for taking a month to prepare a "Master Marketing Plan" before they did any actual publicity work. This sounded like bullshit, and what do you know, it turned out to be bullshit. That whole engagement was a huge waste of money. It generated no useful publicity. Classic parasitic consultants.

Being easy to hire and retain, hard to fire, and acting to lock down your own income regardless of project outcome, makes you vulnerable to accusations of parasitism. And it creates the kinds of moral hazard that make such accusations likely to become true, even if they aren't initially. But it doesn't make such accusations automatically true, just easy to level.

Hard to hire, hard to retain, easy to fire translates into this structural heuristic:

> Rely only on inbound leads to get gigs. Within gigs, never do billable work that you're not explicitly asked to.

For the latter part of the principle, you can always suggest options for various ways to achieve an end (including using your services) that might solve a problem the client has, but the choice is theirs. And you can always give them freebies at your discretion to build trust and goodwill, but the choice to ask for more of the same with pay is theirs.

The client should *never* be surprised by an item on an invoice, or feel like they were forced to sign off on it to get what they actually wanted done (unwanted bundling basically). If you are able to follow this principle 100%, you'll basically have 100% structural immunity to charges of parasitism, because you'll be able to say with honesty (though I've never had to):

You guys sought me out, I've done nothing you didn't ask me to, I'm making no money on autopilot, I'm not bundling in shit you don't want, and you can kick me out any time you like. How am I the parasite?

If you cannot hit 100%, you'll be vulnerable to the extent you're forced to deviate from it. At 100%, you are also well-armed to go on the offensive and cast a spotlight on parasitism elsewhere if the situation calls for it. This can be hard (but not impossible) when you are at less than 100%. Basically putting yourself in the role of "let he who is without sin cast the first stone." Engineering a condition of "no skin in the parasitism game" makes you an honest witness of it.

Should you aim for 100% practical immunity in every gig? Depends on the weakness of the organization and risk profile. You can take calculated risks (and remember this is *reputational* risk that you pay for with character/integrity perceptions that might dog you for years, not mere financial risk within a single gig).

Every outbound pitch, every uninvited speculative proposal, every suggestion within a gig that could be perceived as manufacturing unnecessary billable work for yourself, exposes you to possible accusations that you are exploiting gullible leaders/managers (or colluding with corrupt ones) to parasitically feed on a weak organization.

I personally don't like to play risk management games when it comes to reputation, so I've pretty much stuck to 100% inbound and 100% do-only-what's-asked consulting, with no passive or bundled billables.

I let clients know upfront that they *entirely* control the pace of the engagement and volume of work. I do not set an expected frequency of meetings, a minimum number of hours, or structure gigs to include fixed costs like non-negotiable initial discovery research hours, or ongoing maintenance hours, though in many gigs I've had the leverage or trust to demand such terms and the cash-flow pressures to make it tempting to do so. Occasionally I let clients pay for a block of hours upfront to ease their budgeting, but that's about it as far as deviations from my pay-as-you-go model go.

The only real control I maintain over a gig is prioritization of work requests: I prioritize client requests based on overall volume. If they want deeper, faster engagement from me, they have to *choose* to rely more on me overall. The more you actually rely on me, the more I prioritize what you ask of me, which usually leads to more reliance on me. A virtuous cycle of increasing meaningful entanglement. Conversely, the less they rely on me, the less I prioritize them, a cycle of gradual disengagement.

All this is neither about noble ethics (I'm not particularly noble), nor a subtle rainmaking stunt (as far as I can tell, this rule is a self-imposed tax that lowers my potential income). It is simple self-preservation. As an independent consultant, your reputation for integrity is pretty much the *only* kind of capital you have. And if that gets tarnished, you're done.

You have to either quit the game, or go over to the dark side of self-consciously parasitic consulting. But I don't want that, and neither do you. Because you and I, we're in the game for the intellectual challenges it offers. We're not parasites. Whatever actual parasites say.

---

1. See the interview at www.youtube.com/watch?v=rp6_3UQLi2Y
2. In a large organization, even if you are playing a clean game, doesn't mean other consultants in the organization are.

24

WHAT COLOR IS YOUR HALO?
A HALO SURROUNDS YOU WHEREVER YOU GO

DO you know how you are perceived in a client organization? You've probably heard of the halo effect[1] where a generally positive gestalt is created around things or people with specific positive traits. For example, charismatic and articulate people who project confidence are viewed as more trustworthy and intelligent.

Take a second to think about this question: *what color is your halo?* Or less figuratively, *what do you think is the gestalt effect of how you are perceived in a client organization.* I got the idea for this question from a 1970s job-hunting classic called *What Color is Your Parachute?* According to author Richard Nelson Bolles, the title came about as a joke:

> Years later, Bolles explained the book's memorable title as his response at a business meeting in 1968 when someone told him that he and several co-workers were "bailing out" of a failing organization, prompting Bolles to joke, "What color is your parachute?" "The question was just a joke," he said, "I had no idea that it would take on all this additional meaning."

It is interesting that a precipitate exit from a job in the industrial world is, by default, perceived as a catastrophic failure event that requires a parachute to survive. Even senior executives think in terms of "golden parachutes."

One of the hardest mental shifts to make as an indie is letting go of this catastrophic failure mental model. *You only need a parachute if you think you're in a crashing airplane.* If you don't believe that exiting paycheck employment is like jumping out of an airplane, parachutes are moot. Certainly, there is risk involved in leaping out of paycheck employment, but these days, it is hardly a leaping-out-of-a-plane level of risk. Or if it is, indies leap out not with parachutes, but with wings.

HALOS OVER PARACHUTES

A parachute is for people who might fall to their deaths. Halos are for angels with wings who can float in the air without an organization beneath their feet. Your future depends not on the color of your parachute but the color of your halo. Which is why *what color is your halo?* is a good question for gigworkers. Halos are very important in indie consulting, because they shape how you are perceived when you enter a client organization *as an outsider,* which is very different from entering it as an employee, as you'll have learned if you've been at it for more than a few months.

In consulting work, it is important to be able to recognize a few important types of halos, including your own. A picture of a handful is on the following page.

SALARIED HALOS

Let's take a quick inventory of the five salaried halo types in the picture.

Star employee halo: This is the most basic kind of halo. The star employee harmonizes with the organizational background without blending in, is generally viewed positively, *and sets the internal stan-*

dard by which the halos of external parties are judged. The star
employee is the hero of the organization. The halo color is gold, as
in Golden Boy. I enjoyed a golden-boy halo for a couple of years a
decade ago. It was fun and came with privileges, but it is frankly an
overrated experience, since it tends to create limiting perceptions.

| The variety of business halos

Big consulting firm halo: Employees of big consulting firms are
the main external parties with recognized internal status (contractors and below-the-API staff are generally not seen at all). They
tend to have somewhat robotic, one-size-fits-all, terminator-type
halos. They project a mix of effective professionalism and intimida-
tion (through borrowed authority of the CEO, and perception of
involvement in things like layoffs). Their halo color is blue, as in
blue chip. Big consulting firms are often seen as emissaries of the
broader industry or market. There is a hint of benchmarking and
judgment in the very presence of one of them in your workgroup.

Specialist consultant halo: Specialist consultant types, such as
lawyers or CPAs, tend to be put in well-defined boxes (hence the

square halo). Their halos too are blue, and they too are seen as emissaries of the broader industry or market, but less threatening. They are sometimes indies, but more often part of partnership firms, receiving both paychecks and a share of profits. They often represent a particular sort of risk management, but crucially, they don't *own* the risk, or participate in it. They just help clients manage it.

Auditor/inquisitor halo: Some sorts of outsiders have unambiguous threatening halos: auditors, compliance consultants for health regulations, pollution, sustainability, or diversity, trainers offering sexual harassment seminars, and so on. Their halo color is green, as in *greenlighting* (as in signing off on your compliance/conformity to some sort of external standard), but also as in *greenwashing* (accepting complicity in a theater of compliance, particularly common in sustainability, hence the term).

Charismatic halo: Many charismatic outsiders, such as famous authors, celebrity professors, and ex-presidents, tend to be brought in for largely ceremonial purposes such as keynotes during marquee meetings. They are not there to provoke, rock the boat, or actually make any difference. They are there to lend star power and charisma to the status quo. Their halo is therefore the same color as star employees—golden. Except their halo is actually star-shaped, since they are stars in the broader world outside. Often, they model, in exaggerated form, one or more desirable characteristics the organization wants to encourage in employees. They also afford senior leaders a chance to BIRG—bask in reflected glory.

That's just a sampling of the halos you might see in a typical organization. There are many more, but that should give you an idea of how to think about perceptual gestalts of people against organizational backdrops. Let's talk about the sixth cartoon, the indie halo.

THE INDIE HALO

Now here we run into a problem. Indies come in many varieties. In fact each indie is technically a distinct variety or they wouldn't be called indies. There may be a certain amount of imitation in methods and postures, but we aren't cookie-cutter types.

My opening question—*what color is your halo?*—was a trick question. There is a correct answer: as an indie, your halo should not have a fixed color. This should be obvious if you absorbed the lesson of *A Self-Image is a Dangerous Thing* a few chapters back. The whole point of indie status is a certain amount of adaptability.

The default mode of indie consulting is to adapt to a very specific situation. Sometimes this means projecting confidence and charisma. Other times, it means projecting a narrow kind of competence. And sometimes it means projecting an annoying Jiminy Cricket type of conscience-on-the-shoulder personality.

You can never tell until you're *in* the situation what the right way to play it is. This is in part because indie consulting, no matter what you do, nearly always has a strongly improvisational component to it. You have to go *yes, and . . .* in response to the opening overtures of the client. And the nature of that improv response depends on the nature of the situation and the posture the client is adopting within it. Your task is often to provide a response that is surprising without being disruptive.

If you're new to this, one trick is to spot the local star employee halo and then play foil to them in an interesting way. You don't want to be seen as competing with the local hero, nor as the natural villain opposed to them. *You want to be seen as someone whose presence makes the local hero's journey more interesting.* If you're lucky, that local hero is in fact your client. If not, it's a trickier improv challenge.

It takes time and practice across many situations and with many clients to develop a broad halo range, but once you've expanded beyond a couple of basic postures, you'll find that it gets easier and easier.

So take another stab at answering the question: *what color is your halo?* But this time, instead of a single color and shape, think of the *ranges* of colors and shapes your halo might span, and how you might expand them.

---

1. en.wikipedia.org/wiki/Halo_effect

SECTION FIVE

MENTAL FITNESS

Strong people are harder to kill than weak people and more useful in general.

MARK RIPPETOE

25

BASIC CONSULTANT DIAGRAMS
I DIAGRAM THEREFORE I AM

THIS IS a chapter on basic consulting diagrams—the kinds of diagrams that you should be able to instinctively judge as appropriate to a discussion and rapidly whiteboard without thinking too hard. I've included sixteen of my favorites in the diagram on the next page to get you started, but you should develop your own vocabulary.

Recent chats with some friends have made me realize that my approach to consulting is based on what academics call ethnomethodology[1] and this particularly applies to how I use diagrams in conversations. Loosely, ethnomethodology means taking the modes of thought and problem solving of lay people seriously, and in my case, actually making them my own.

A great deal of business thinking runs on diagrams drawn on whiteboards or inserted into presentations and briefings. There is usually a good reason actual working people doing serious work rely on these diagrams to frame and structure conversations. You're not a good consultant until you understand the logic and appeal of every popular diagram and learn to use each tastefully.

A word on the relationship between diagramming approaches and indie consulting brands: Many beginning consultants have a weird kind of insecurity that leads them to invent and rely on over-complicated, bespoke constructs that they can name after themselves. While these can sometimes be useful, especially ones that are developed and refined over many years, across hundreds of applications, such as Wardley mapping (a diagramming technique developed by Simon Wardley), in general, they are fragile visual bullshit. You're mostly better off learning to use the basic diagrams well than trying to make up and sell your own.

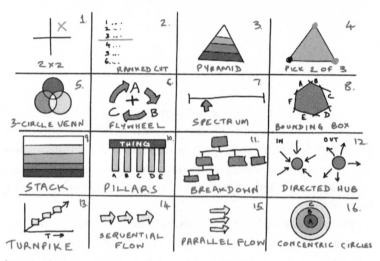

| Basic consulting diagrams

Many consultants also seem to take a weird kind of pride in avoiding the basic tools of the consulting trade, like 2x2 diagrams, almost as though they are afraid they won't be taken seriously if they use such familiar constructs. To me, this is a clear tell that you don't have confidence in your basic thinking and so are wary of commodity packaging. That, or you're exhibiting a kind of snobbery towards vernacular visual business language that will lead to people distrusting you and refusing to think with you.

Of course, a few people genuinely have objections to one or other diagramming approach as representing dangerously sloppy thinking. Simon Wardley and I have a long-running good-natured beef about 2x2s for example. But he's also the creator of one of the best 2x2s I've seen: openness *vs.* level of strategic play.

Basic diagrams are basic for a reason. They're like free weights in the consulting gym. Sure they can be used in cringe-inducing ways that are vulnerable to parody, but used with good form, they blow complicated name-brand machine weights and fancy equipment out of the water. Whatever kind of consulting you do, it pays to master basic consulting diagrams. What is common to all of these is that you do not need external data, measurements, or generally even a brainstorm. These are ways to capture your *existing* situation awareness of what's going on, and structure the conversation in a way that participants can pool their beliefs, with the right dominant mood (such as conflict, cooperation, analysis, or synthesis).

All sixteen of these diagrams also have a very special and useful feature: they can usually be described with 5–9 chunks of information. This fits Miller's famous Magic Number argument[2] that we can hold 7±2 items in short-term memory. This means good discussions tend to stay in that range and avoid the meeting getting stupid.

Let's take a quick tour of the sixteen basic diagrams.

1. THE 2X2

The 2x2 is the barbell squat in the business gym. Basic and cliché, but a full-brain workout that forces you to think, pay attention, and practice good form to avoid injury. It can be used to break out of a zero-sum situation by adding a dimension, relate archetypal cases, etc. One of its most interesting and unexpected uses is as a conflict de-escalation tool. When two people are arguing about mutually exclusive options, or a single spectrum, moving the conversation to

a non-conflict mode (if that's what you
want to do) can be as simple as adding an
axis that makes the unspoken conflict vari-
able explicit. The 2x2 is also a natural sweet
spot. Resist the temptation to go 3x3 or
2x2x2. It almost never works. Get good at
the 2x2.

| The 2x2

Miller complexity: 11 // two axis labels,
four limit labels, four quadrant labels, one title

Examples: BCG Growth Share matrix, Johari window

2. THE RANKED CUT

If the 2x2 is the squat, the ranked cut is the
deadlift. A simple list is just a data-capture
structure, but what makes the ranked cut a
proper diagram is the addition of a single
line, to model a cut-off or threshold.
Usually you get to a ranked cut by brainstorming a list, ranking it in some priority
order, and then having a discussion about

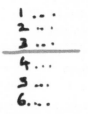

| The Ranked Cut

where to draw the line and why (which can lead to revision in the
prioritization logic). The line usually marks a proposal dividing
different regimes of action (in the simplest case, *do vs. don't*).

Miller complexity: 4 // above the line, below the line, meaning of
the line, ranking criterion

Examples: feature prioritization, candidates shortlisting

3. THE PYRAMID

The pyramid is used to illustrate a leverage
hierarchy of some sort. It is perhaps the
most familiar diagram, and is synonymous
with organizations themselves. The basic

| The Pyramid

use of the pyramid is to create a hierarchical structural scaffolding to identify levels of abstraction in analysis, description, or prescription. It's a blank map template for anything. I of course, love pyramids. My entire consulting career is based on an essay about one: Hugh MacLeod's sociopaths-clueless-losers pyramid.

Miller complexity: 3 to 7

Examples: Capability Maturity Model, Maslow's pyramid, MacLeod hierarchy

4. THE PICK-2-OF-3 TRIANGLE

The pick-2-of-3 is probably my own favorite after the 2x2, but is not very commonly used, and this is primarily because it is among the most difficult to use. It requires thinking about interacting real-world constraints that model real tradeoffs. It is an excellent tool to use when

| The Pick-2-of-3 Triangle

people seem to be forgetting constraints that matter and are going wild with too-sloppy brainstorming. As with 2x2s, there seems to be a natural limit and a sweet-spot value to the 2-of-3 case, and attempts to create *n*-of-*m* discussions generally don't work, so don't go nuts trying. The combinatorics just get too out of hand and exit the Miller 7 +/-2 zone fast.

Miller complexity: 3 to 6 // three basic constraint variables, three pairwise-active regimes

Examples: the original cheap/fast/good pizza triangle, the Mundell-Fleming trilemma, the CAP theorem

5. THE 3-CIRCLE VENN DIAGRAM

The Venn diagram is a way to create an interference pattern, and add resolution to a basic structure by creating a set of fill-in-the-blank complexities. The three-circle Venn diagram is the most common one for a good reason: all possible intersections create zones. When you get up to four, you can't intersect opposite pairs pairwise visually. Venn diagrams are particularly useful for arche-type analysis, where traits intersect in interesting ways to create evocative role descriptions, like the famous geeks-dweebs-dorks Venn diagram.[3]

The 3-Circle Venn Diagram

Miller complexity: 10 // seven mutually exhaustive regions, three basic circle labels

Examples: geeks-dweebs-dorks diagram, Drew Conway data science diagram[4]

6. THE FLYWHEEL

The flywheel is a visualization of a system that creates compounding effects via a positive feedback loop or virtuous cycle. It is a diagram that is powerful in inverse proportion to the number of blocks in the positive-feedback circle. A 2-block flywheel is more powerful than a 3-block flywheel.

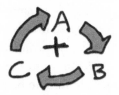

The Flywheel

Negative feedback flywheels are also useful to visualize draining momentum/vicious cycles.

Miller complexity: 2 to 7 // one per block in the circle

Examples: Customer acquisition loops, Amazon flywheel

7. THE SPECTRUM

The spectrum is probably the single most commonly used business diagram, but is easily my least favorite because it tends to suck people into a no-exit, zero-sum frame.

The Spectrum

Often, people use sets of spectra to characterize a large decision space or flesh out the feature space of a product category. This is a slightly better way to use spectra. Spectra can be binary or continuous and the resulting "product spaces" defined by spectra can be a mix of discrete and continuous.

The spectrum is probably more useful in discussions about design problems than analysis problems.

Miller complexity: 3 per spectrum // end points, pointer position

Examples: feature set descriptions for disruption debates, persona models

8. THE BOUNDING BOX

The bounding box is one of my favorites, but I rarely see non-engineers use it. It is a loose, qualitative generalization of the idea of a design space, illustrating the zone where you have freedom of choice. Each edge—and I recommend drawing bounding boxes as irregular polygons—represents

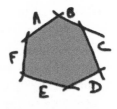

| The Bounding Box

one boundary with an adjacent zone that can affect what you do, but is outside your control. These could be supply chain partners, regulators, etc. For example, in the semiconductor industry, if you are a chip-design company, you might have a bounding box with foundry, device manufacturers, and IP partners as your edges.

Miller complexity: 4 to 9 // three to eight labeled boundary edges, with an interior label for your in-scope design space

Examples: diagrams of supply-chains, diagrams of physics constraints affecting a design

9. THE STACK

The stack is another diagram inherited from engineering, with the archetype being the stack diagram of a computer. It looks a bit like the pyramid, but has equal size layers. It is great to use for discussing actual stacks involved in engineering, design, and architecture discussions, as well as more abstract things like industry-sector structure, and market structure.

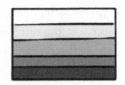

| The Stack

Miller complexity: 3 to 7 // I've rarely seen stack diagrams with > seven layers

Examples: industry-structure diagrams, software architectures

10. THE PILLARS

The pillars are, to me, one of the most interesting diagram types because I almost never use them. Their sweet spot is *values-based reasoning.* This does not necessarily mean ethics at a human level. It can be a dogma for highly opinionated engineering

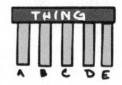

| The Pillars

design. The vertical orientation suggests a cutting-through of a stack or pyramid, and each pillar suggests a "present at every level of abstraction" concept. So pillars necessarily have to be somewhat abstract because they'll be embodied differently at different levels. With three-pillar diagrams, you can also discuss stability questions, since a two-legged stool will fall over.

Miller complexity: 3 to 6 // more than six pillars and you have a caterpillar

Examples: "core values" diagrams, equilibrium diagrams

11. THE BREAKDOWN

The breakdown is a special kind of top-down tree, where a large ambiguous thing is progressively broken down into component parts that are bite-sized chunks ready for resource allocation, responsibility assignment, or functional coverage in a

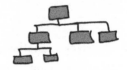

| The Breakdown

design. They can be used in formal, technical ways in some engineering disciplines, but are commonly used in much more informal ways.

Miller complexity: 9 to 15 // with some chunking by branch and level lowering the cognitive burden to single digits

Examples: project breakdown, root cause analysis, org charts

12. THE DIRECTED SPOKES

The directed spokes are a set of arrows arranged along the spokes of an imaginary wheel, with a labeled hub. In an inward pointing orientation, they usually represent environmental forces you must respond to.

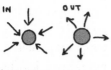

| The Directed Spokes

In the less-common outward orientation, they represent some sort of impact analysis. Where a flow (see 14 and 15) is a controlled, directed pattern of unfolding action and consequences, the outward spokes are good for thinking about relatively uncontrolled impact patterns, such as the effects of a major press release.

Miller complexity: 4 to 5 // 1 per spoke, 1 central concept

Examples: descriptions of environmental factors affecting a company, convergence/divergence in trends, impact analysis, fallout patterns

13. THE TURNPIKE

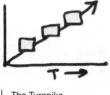

The turnpike is an idealized pattern of growth where two evolving variables are in a healthy dynamic balance. In the simplest, somewhat degenerate case, the x-axis is

| The Turnpike

simply time, while the y-axis is something like capability. The turnpike—the term is from economics—is the vector of optimal growth. Below the line and above the line you get some sort of suboptimal (and possibly unstable) out-of-balance condition. On the turnpike, you get some sort of idealized pattern of evolution or growth.

Miller complexity: 7 to 9 // one per axis, turnpike label, above/below line region labels, one per "milestone" box

Examples: product development roadmaps, capability maturation paths, business-evolution stages

14. THE SEQUENTIAL FLOW

The sequential flow is a *single* set of arrows going from left to right, representing the temporal gestalt. The more detailed (and in most cases, less useful and possibly harm-

| The Sequential Flow

ful) version is the Gantt chart. The sequential flow *serializes* the necessarily complex detailed behavior into a set of phases or gears. Often separated by stage gates with go/no-go decision points, in which case this is the horizontal, temporal version of the ranked cut.

Miller complexity: 3 to 8 // one per arrow, and, optionally, one between each pair of arrows, and a pair of bookends, along with a overall flow label

Examples: project phase structure, narrative structure, causal hypotheses

15. THE PARALLEL FLOW

Parallel-flow diagrams are useful when you need to talk about synchronized efforts. Unlike the vertically oriented cousin (*10. Pillars*) which represent timeless values, the parallel flow represents the most precisely timed artifact in business: the synchroniza-

| The Parallel Flow

tion point. Things that have to line up at a single point in time.

Usually it is used to talk about an all-or-nothing outcome with several necessary conditions (a large *AND* gate basically); with some practice you can also use it for talking about hedged option sets (an *OR* gate).

Miller complexity: 3 to 8 // one per arrow, synchronization point label, overall flow label

Examples: launch conditions modeling, go/no-go necessary/sufficient conditions

16. THE CONCENTRIC CIRCLES

The last of my sixteen basic diagrams is a focusing tool. Concentric circles are usually used to think about fuzzy structural boundaries, with a stepped transition from inside to outside. A common example is modeling an ecosystem or sets of prioritized concerns with a coarse ordering. The

| The Concentric Circles

concentric circles are closely related to the basic linear spectrum. The radial axis of a concentric circles diagram is a directed spectrum. The tangential direction represents an unsorted residual direction of "everything else."

Miller complexity: 3 to 5 // one per ring

Examples: ecosystem models, partitioning of concerns along a focal to peripheral spectrum

USING VISUAL LANGUAGE

There are plenty more, but I'll stop at sixteen. Diagrams are like any other language. You get better with practice and your vocabulary expands as you gain both experience and theoretical knowledge. As long as you never use diagrams simply for the sake of using them, and focus on improving your ability to pattern match contexts where a particular type of diagram is useful, your command of the language will improve and you will become more eloquent and useful as a discussion partner.

Don't turn your nose up at the basic stuff. Don't invent or use unnecessary, bespoke, complex stuff. Use what works, pay attention to *when* and *how* it works, and use it better next time. If people you're talking to seem to have an aversion to particular bits of your vocabulary, don't waste too much time trying to convince them. Just switch to mutually preferred vocabulary. The point is the discussion, not displaying your diagramming prowess. It's not complicated unless you want to make it complicated.

---

1. en.wikipedia.org/wiki/Ethnomethodology
2. en.wikipedia.org/wiki/The_Magical_Number_Seven,_Plus_or_Minus_Two
3. laughingsquid.com/nerd-venn-diagram-geek-dork-or-dweeb/
4. drewconway.com/zia/2013/3/26/the-data-science-venn-diagram

26

TRAINING YOUR NERVES

AS A FREE AGENT, YOUR NERVES MATTER MORE THAN YOUR SKILLS

AN IDEA I've cited often in the last few years is Arthur C. Clarke's "hazards of prophecy," from his book *Profiles of the Future,* which asserts that failure of nerve is a bigger problem than failure of imagination. Failure of nerve happens when, despite being given all the facts, and despite the required reasoning being trivial, people fail to draw obvious conclusions about the future. The problem is that the simple reasoning from simple premises leads you towards an unpleasant conclusion that's hard to face.

Before one attempts to set up in business as a prophet, it is instructive to see what success others have made of this dangerous occupation—and it is even more instructive to see where they have failed. With monotonous regularity, apparently competent men have laid down the law about what is technically possible or impossible—and have been proved utterly wrong, sometimes while the ink was scarcely dry from their pens. On careful analysis, it appears that these debacles fall into two classes, which I will call "failures of nerve" and "failures of imagination." The failure of nerve seems to be the more common; it occurs when even given all the relevant facts the would-be prophet cannot see that they point to an inescapable conclusion. Some of these failures are so ludicrous as to be almost unbelievable, and would form an interesting subject for psychological analysis, "They said it couldn't be done" is a phrase that occurs throughout the history of invention [. . .]

This is an important phenomenon for us in the gig economy to recognize. Possibly the most basic level of failure in failed gig economy careers is failure of nerve.

FIRST LEAP *VS.* *N*TH LEAP

It's obvious that taking your first leap into the gig economy, especially when you're not being forced to by circumstances, is an act of courage. In large part though, the courage required there is a kind of dutch courage, except that you're high on the prospect of freedom rather than alcohol. You don't actually know much yet about the perils you're diving into, or what kind of courage you will need, as you plan your first leap (see Part III on that). You're merely assuming you have it.

The courage it takes is based on a belief similar to "I'm smart enough to graduate college" or "I'm strong enough to lift this weight." It's a belief that allows you to try, but it may not be enough for you to succeed. It is a belief that you *will* have the courage necessary when it is actually called for.

Such beliefs fuel a kind of false confidence that relies on ignorance, but can bootstrap you into the real thing. You find out how you actually stack up as tests of such beliefs hit you one after the other. By the time you're on your *n*th leap, your courage is real because it is in response to dangers you *do* understand.

TRAINING NERVES *VS.* MITIGATING RISKS

Like intelligence or strength, courage is an attribute that can be trained, refined, specialized, and generally matured into a knowledge-based understanding of what one is actually capable of. As with intelligence and strength, most people are far away from the genetic limit of what they might be capable of.

But training your nerves is not the same thing as reducing the risk itself through risk-mitigating skills. A good example is the difference between learning to swim and learning to jump off the high board. Learning to swim takes no courage at all if you do it in the shallow end, under skilled supervision. You can get to swimming safely without ever testing your nerves, or ever having to overcome even a moment of panic, by gradually developing your skills.

On the other hand, assuming you know how to swim, learning to jump (not dive) off the high board takes no skill at all. You just have to step off the board and fall. It's all about raw nerve. It's about learning to overcome the fear itself, accepting that knot in your stomach and the sudden rush of weird sensations as you step off. And it's almost a one-step thing: the second time is far easier, and by the tenth time, you're actually enjoying the thrill.

Learning to function effectively as a paycheck employee does not take much nerve, but does take a lot of specialized employer-specific skills you can learn in the shallow end of the pool. If the organization is well run, it should be like learning to swim with a good teacher. If it isn't, you'll drown.

Learning to function effectively as a free agent, on the other hand, takes a lot more nerve, but generally no additional skills beyond what you already have. It's like learning to jump off the high board repeatedly till you enjoy rather than dread it.

To the extent there are risks, you don't actually mitigate them much. You just learn to deal with the consequences of environments with unmanaged, unmitigated risks.

DIMENSIONS OF BOLDNESS

Though you can't train your nerves in the same way you train skills that de-risk an activity, you *can* train them. What you're learning is to act in certain ways despite unpleasant visceral responses getting in the way.

It helps to break it down a bit into aspects. Here's a spider chart of the nerves I think matter most in the gig economy. The solid polygon is a sketch of what I think my own pattern of boldness looks like. The dotted one is the pattern I think a fictional nemesis of mine, Arnie Anscombe, data science consultant, exhibits. Relative to him, I'm bolder about trusting my gut, adapting fast, and ending things cleanly, while he's bolder at committing early and recovering fast from setbacks. You should try drawing your own.

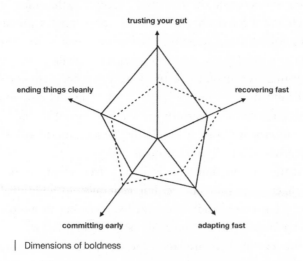

| Dimensions of boldness

Along each spoke is a dimension of courage associated with a particular pattern of failure of nerve. In each case, you lose opportunities, time, or both. Lose enough of both, and you lose the plot entirely, and bomb out of the gig economy.

Failure to trust your gut: When things seem okay on the surface, but there are a couple of red flags and something just seems wrong at gut level, you either trust your gut and poke at the red flags to either confirm or allay your suspicions, or you studiously ignore your gut.

Failure to recover fast: You will routinely have setbacks with immediate and unpleasant impacts. A gig fails to come through. An invoice gets held up, causing a cash-flow crunch. A sudden medical emergency stresses your reserves. In each case, if your nerve fails, you'll initially freeze into helpless inaction, wondering why the universe is being so damn unfair to you. The failure of nerve happens when you don't unfreeze and begin acting again quickly enough.

Failure to adapt fast: Circumstances have changed. The CEO was replaced and your champion at a client company who was going to send a nice juicy gig your way is suddenly out of power or out of a job. Do you reorient quickly and do something about it or wait just long enough that the loss becomes irrecoverable?

Failure to commit early: You have an idea you feel is basically ready to be tried. You've workshopped it a bit on Twitter. People are excited and seem positively disposed towards it. But you delay and hedge, and don't act, and when you're finally ready, the moment of zeitgeist resonance has passed. You're too late or someone else gets there first.

Failure to end things cleanly: A potential client has been stringing you along forever. But you don't cut the conversation short as a waste of time and move on. Or a client who you thought represented tens of hours a month in billings is only sending 1-2 hours a quarter your way, but demanding a level of support and situation awareness maintenance that you can only justify for much higher volumes. But you're letting the gig limp along instead of just politely ending it.

All these cases are failures of nerve. The situation is not intricate or hard to read. The outcome of the present course of inaction is obvious and bad. It is obvious what to do instead, to try and create a better outcome.

Yet you don't act. Failure of nerve. The horror of recognizing that something isn't working, or that a comforting belief isn't true, or that something important has changed.

The good news about failure of nerve is that it cannot become a habit. If your nerve fails you often enough, you'll just fail entirely and drop out of the gig economy into something else (generally more unpleasant).

What *can* become a habit is acting with nerve. And that takes no real skill. Just doing the thing that obviously needs doing. And doing it again, and again. Until the panic reaction turns into an exhilaration reaction.

The reason this works is obvious: the riskiest thing you can do is to take no risks at all. Every time you act with courage, and avert a failure of nerve, you rebalance luck in your favor. You start being right more often. You attract more serendipity than zemblanity.

[1]In fact, that's how you know if you're acting boldly enough. When you start to feel that you're getting unreasonably lucky, and more of your bets are paying off than you'd have expected.

The idea that "fortune favors the bold" is not an observation about the nature of divine agency, it is an observation about the interaction of active *human* agency, luck, and unintended consequences. Fortune appears to favor the bold because the bold are making their own luck by acting in obvious ways in response to obvious imperatives. Failure of nerve is so common, it is almost the default, so even doing marginally better than others pays off. As Wayne Gretzky succinctly put it, you miss 100% of the shots you don't take.

---

1. Zemblanity is the opposite of serendipity, defined as "unsurprisingly unlucky."

27

THE IMPORTANCE OF BEING SURPRISABLE

THE SUPERPOWER OF INDIE CONSULTANTS IS OPENNESS TO SURPRISE

WE'VE TALKED a lot about four types of economic entities in this book: big organizations, startups, under-the-API gigworkers such as rideshare drivers, and finally our core class—independent consultants. The superficial structural differences are obvious, but what are the *real*, deep differences that account for their different economic roles and mutual relationships? I'm going to try and explain it with two pictures.

The first picture is a generic Venn diagram of organizational behavior modes that applies to all four (considering free agents to be one-person organizations). All organizational behavior can be understood in terms of the intersections of *problems, resources,* and *surprises,* which intersect to create seven behavioral zones like in the diagram on the next page.

I'll let you think about my seven behavioral zones on your own, but I want to make a couple of general comments before zooming in on the indie consulting version.

The first thing to recognize about the diagram is that problems and resources don't have to match/overlap much, but do need to be approximately equal in magnitude, so you can balance them via creative trade and commerce with outside parties. Bullshit work usually indicates underutilized capacities that can be sold to others. Futile gestures and signaling generally indicate real problems that could be solved by third parties. If the scope of opportunities to spend/make money are evenly matched, there is the possibility of gradually increasing the efficiency zone.

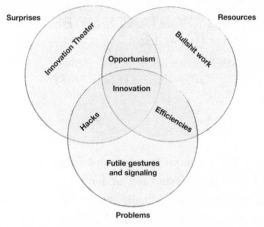

| Organizational behaviors

But if your problems sum to $1 billion and your resources sum to $100k, there's a basic mismatch that cannot be solved without some true innovation and probably brute-force capitalization. More likely, you will simply try to shrink the scope of the problems you accept to match the resources you have, or die trying.

The second thing to recognize is the role surprises play in shaping organizational behavior. Good/bad doesn't matter. Sometimes unexpected gifts turn out to be curses. Other times, making lemonade from lemons turns out to be a huge win. What matters is that something unexpected has entered your world from the vast unknown outside.

I'm something of an extremist on this point. I believe nothing truly significant ever changes in an organization without the injection of a surprise from the external world, followed by a creative and imaginative internal response to it. Surprises are necessary (but not sufficient) fuel for growth and change.

Without a stream of external surprises in the picture, the problems-resources relationship is generally in a zero-sum gridlock and doesn't offer much opportunity to break out of bad situations. All you can hope for is slow, painstaking growth or decline driven by conscious discipline.

But external surprises can break the gridlock. Whether in positive or negative ways is partly, but not entirely, up to you. Organizations differ in their "surprisal surface area," both in terms of the scope of generally salient surprises, and the degree of direct overlap between the stream of surprises and the resource/problem gridlock picture.

VARIETIES OF SURPRISABILITY

The trick to understanding different types of organizations is recognizing that these circles and intersection zones are sized differently for our four basic types. And of course we can plot them on a 2x2. What I've plotted here are typical representatives of each class.

See what's going on here? Big organizations and under-the-API gigworkers are both *process* constrained. This means relatively low scope for relevant surprises (small lightly shaded circle), and weak ability to respond to them (small overlap zone).

Startups and under-the-API gigworkers are both *resource-limited,* which means there is a significant mismatch between the scale of problems they have to take on and the resources they have available to address them (darkest circle bigger than medium shaded circle). This means the situation is unsustainable long term without some differential growth or shrinkage to balance the two. Startups and gigworkers are both in grow-or-die mode and the growth is required as much to right-shape their economic roles as to make them profitable.

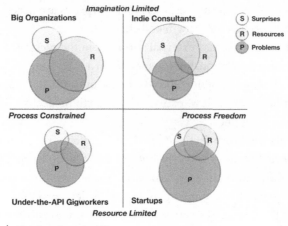

| Varieties of surprisability

But indie consultants are unique among the four types in having a *much* bigger surprisal surface area and overlap zones than the other three. We are neither process constrained like under-the-API gigworkers, nor faced with a severe mismatch between resources and problems like startups. So we can afford to sustain a very significant openness to surprisal, and a much higher ability to solve problems in ways *besides* arguing over resources with others.

THE ART OF BEING SURPRISABLE

A trivial example: if you're reasonably smart and broadly curious and interested in stuff, almost any item in the news can be fodder for something like a blog post or quick-turnaround expertise acquisition if you want to invest more time.

These can then be turned into money fairly easily, with mechanisms ranging from subscription newsletters and online classes, to corporate workshops or spec work for appropriately targeted clients. This means you can respond to a *lot* more of what's going on in the world than the other three types of organizations. *This is the reason the main product a lot of indie consultants sell is surprises transformed into customized/personalized action optionality for clients.* Because we have surplus capacity to respond to surprises ourselves, we sell that capacity to others who have a deficit, due to process or resource limitations.

Startups are equally process-unconstrained, but their capacity for surprisal is limited by the fact that they are trying to build out one very specific ambitious thing with very scarce resources, so their lightly shaded circle of relevant surprises is smaller. Otoh, big companies have a lot of resources, but are too constrained by their processes to ingest significant surprisal. Under-the-API gigworkers, of course, are the most constrained of all.

You need five things going on to turn surprisability into economic leverage:

1. *Openness to experience:* You have to be paying attention outside your focal zones and, ideally, actively provoking parts of the environment to generate surprise-fuel for yourself.
2. *Depth of curiosity:* A surprise by itself is like rain. Without adequate forest cover and porous soil, it just flows away like a flash flood. To trap surprise in the form of an asset, you need a rich and broad awareness of the world so you can integrate surprising new things into things you already know/do in interesting ways.
3. *Lack of missionary lock:* Your life should *not* be built around a single overarching mission to the degree that you can't react opportunistically in ways unrelated to other things you are doing. If you have that kind of lock, you need to turn yourself into a startup.
4. *Imagination:* Cultivate the ability to see the possibilities latent in a surprise that are within your zone of actionability. Nobody else can do this for you. This is a kind of connecting of dots that relies on your private knowledge.

5. *Boldness:* The ability to overcome doubts and just act to
   be the agent of whatever the environment has enabled to
   happen. The ability to say: this connection is just waiting
   to be made, somebody has to make it, why not me?

That's ODLIB if you like mnemonics: **o**penness to experience,
depth of curiosity, **l**ack of missionary lock, **i**magination, **b**oldness.

If you think your surprisability is weak, you might want to start
a surprise log in a notebook or even as an evolving thread of
tweets. Sensitizing yourself to surprise is not hard. Be careful not
to turn it into an idea log though. It's important to learn to see the
surprise itself and the potential it opens up, and not jump too
quickly to a way to do something with it (and most of the time you
won't be able to). That's the only way you'll train your
surprisability.

Pro-tip: a surprise doesn't have to be a new development or
seem obviously surprising at first glance. It just has to be newly
surprising to you, via an insight. It can even be something that
didn't happen ("the dog that didn't bark"). A surprise stream is not a
news feed.

28

YOUR PASSION MISSION

ARRANGING YOUR MONEY-MAKING AROUND YOUR SOUL-FEEDING

WHEN I QUIT my job in 2011, I did so in large part to gain more control over my life so I could devote more time and energy to my writing. Contrary to what many of my readers seemed to assume at the time, the consulting was meant to sustain the writing, not the other way around. If I had stayed on the corporate track I was on, with growing managerial-leadership responsibilities, the writing would have fallen by the wayside long ago.

I suspect most people who *voluntarily* enter the gig economy are like me: they do so in part to gain more control over their lives so they can devote time and energy to a specific passion mission, and bring it into greater harmony with their money-making hustle. Way back in 2009, Hugh Macleod of Gaping Void called this the "Sex and Cash" theory.[1]

> The creative person basically has two kinds of jobs: One is the sexy, creative kind. Second is the kind that pays the bills. Sometimes the assignment covers both bases, but not often.

Sex-and-cash theory is how adults pursue passions. The lazy, feel-good advice to young graduates to "pursue your passion" is rightly derided as entitled trustie[2] bullshit. Typical passions are not a natural fit for the basic life challenges of survival, financial success, social success, status, or recognition.

In fact, linking a passion too directly, and too early, to those things (a particular temptation for those with clear talents related to their passions) is often a surefire way to kill it. The primary purpose of a passion is to feed your soul, not your wallet.

In the short term, passions are generally in a zero-sum relationship with survival. But in the long term, if you don't pursue your passions at all, you won't find life worth living, so the question of survival will become moot.

PASSION AS POSITIVE EXTERNALITY

The trick to pursuing your passion is engineering the right kind of coupling between the "sex" and "cash" parts of your life.

This is becoming easier thanks to vastly improved tools and products, but the fundamentals are not going to change anytime soon: for all but a small fraction of creators, passion and money-making will never align perfectly and will require a thoughtfully engineered coupling to sustain. Hugh MacLeod's point from 2009 —"Sometimes the assignment covers both bases, but not often"— remains as true today.

So a passion economy as such does not exist. The passion part of life still has to emerge, for most of us, as a positive externality from the more pragmatic, money-focused activities of life. Your passion mission may have a certain amount of natural economic potential (which newer tools help realize more easily), but typically not enough to be self-sustaining.

Take a moment to identify your passion mission (if you don't have one you should be worried): it might be a traditional creative activity like writing, music, film-making, or game design. It may or may not have a pathway for "breaking into" the industry devoted to that activity if one exists. It might be a maker/builder project that could turn into a startup. Or not. It might simply be something like building a log cabin in the woods with your own hands, and developing an off-grid lifestyle around it. Don't let apparent financial upside fool you. Just because your passion is something money-related, like say investing and markets, doesn't mean you'll get rich off it. A great screenwriter probably has a better shot at making it big in Hollywood than an amateurish investor has of making it big on Wall Street, going up against the pros.

Whatever your passion mission, it is the *raison d'être* of your indie life or even life overall. The reason you're giving up the security and ease of the paycheck life. The activity into which you're going to be sinking all the freedom you earn through your money-making hustles.

PASSION MISSION STARTUP PAINS

Passion missions typically extend past single projects, like writing a single book or screenplay, or completing a single hardware hacking project. They are activity streams you want to sustain indefinitely, whether or not they turn out to be financially self-sustaining. Which means you need a system. The first thing that happens when you go indie is that your existing systems around your passion mission get shot to pieces. Your passion mission will almost certainly *temporarily* fall by the wayside, as you scramble to get better systems in place to navigate the much more volatile world of free agent money-making.

The transient pains will make you second guess yourself: did you in fact do the right thing? Did you end up sacrificing your passion mission while foolishly imagining you were making more room for it? The second-guessing and doubts are justified, because indeed, that can happen. For hobbyist levels of creative ambition, a steady paycheck job that you're not too ambitious about, with free evenings and weekends, is a much better setup. If you're serious and want to take your passion mission places, the indie life situation is definitely a far better environment for it, *once you do the things necessary to make it work.* It won't happen magically. The making-it-work goes both ways. The passion mission has to inject soul into the money-making activity, and the money-making activity has to be artfully arranged around the core creative disciplines of the passion mission. Either both are sustainable long-term, or neither is.

And you heard that right: *you arrange the money-making around the passion work, not the other way around.* You try to reserve your most alert and creative days and hours for the passion work. The passion work sets the constraints within which the money-making has to work out. In the beginning this is hard. A weekends-and-evenings hobby, arranged around an easy 9-to-5 job of forty hours a week, easily amounts to about sixteen hours a week (say one to two hours every weekday evening, eight hours on the weekend). You can get a lot done in that kind of time. I did the first few years of my blogging this way.

When you are starting up, on the other hand, everything gets in the way. When you're not hustling hard to make money, you're doing more household chores because you have less cash. Plus there's the general background anxiety. So in the first year or so, your passion-mission time availability might plummet to just a few hours a week and they won't be high quality. Even if you saved up a lot of launch money, the anxiety of the runway eventually running out will contaminate the freedom to work on your passion mission. Passion missions are best fed with sustainable time and money surpluses, not by drawing down savings.

Slowly, as you stabilize in your new life, you'll reach a new equilibrium where you can spend a lot more time, in terms of both quality and quantity, on your passion mission. The passion mission can become your actual job. Writing for me today is a 9-to-5 weekday thing, not an evenings-and-weekends thing.

Getting to such a state requires ongoing mindful introspection. Here are some questions to help you get started:

- How do you sustain a shipping discipline around your passion mission?
- What is the difference between a hobby and a passion mission?
- How do you model and engineer the coupling to moneymaking?
- What kind of ambitions should you harbor for your passion mission?
- Is there an ideal sex/cash balance, and if so, how do you get there?
- How does the balance evolve over time?
- What is the deeper yin-yang coupling between the two?

----

1. www.gapingvoid.com/blog/2013/08/06/sex-cash-theory/
2. *Trustie* is an American slang term for young people with significant trust funds.

SECTION SIX

EXECUTIVE SPARRING

A concluding set of essays unpacking my own core business model.

29

INTRODUCTION TO EXECUTIVE SPARRING

A SERIES ABOUT SPARRING-BASED CONSULTING

FOR A WHILE NOW, several of my fellow indie consultants have been asking me to share more details about executive sparring, a style of 1:1 consulting that I've been developing and practicing for almost a decade now. Before I get into it, I recommend watching some sparring videos on YouTube, to get a visceral sense of what I'm going to be talking about.

At their most intense, executive sparring sessions can feel like the intellectual equivalent of physical sparring. Not all sessions are this intense, or this combative, but the most valuable ones—both for me and for the client—are. Like a sparring partner in boxing, an executive sparring partner would not last very long in the ring in an actual competitive bout with a high-functioning executive client. Yet a good sparring partner can provide a great deal of value in a non-bout sparring session.

At this point, I've worked as a sparring partner with several dozen senior executive clients (some of them for years) in organizations ranging from startup scale to Fortune 100 corporations, and across half a dozen industries. Sparring work now constitutes almost the entirety of my consulting practice. It's a fairly demanding and intensive kind of highly personalized 1:1 support work, and is neither cheap, nor very scalable. So unlike things like training workshops, or process/capability consulting, it's not the kind of thing you can offer at scale. You're not going to rack up hundreds or thousands of clients in a few years. You're not going to be sparring with an auditorium-scale audience. Writing a book about your business ideas won't make it any more efficient. You're not going to be automating any of it.

I estimate that a good sparring partner can support no more than half a dozen active clients in any given month without burning out. And it typically takes half a dozen meetings of 60-90 minutes over about six months for the sessions to become truly high value. Most importantly, though you might be able to bill at a high rate, due to the individualized, automation-resistant, time-intensive nature of it, you're not going to get mega-rich doing it. Sparring is an artisanal kind of consulting. You can make a decent living from it, but if you're solving for big money from a 4-hour work week, you should look to a different kind of consulting business model.

TEACHING SPARRING

In late 2021, after conducting an informal sparring workshop for a few friends, I decided I was finally ready to write about it.

While this series is primarily going to be for indie consultants who want to do this for money, it should also be of value to executives, since a significant part of being a leader is serving as sparring partner to peer executives and senior reports. In fact, most sparring happens among peers within organizations or industries. Executives hire people like me mostly when they cannot find suitable sparring partners within their own organizations or institutional neighborhoods—which is as it should be.

Sparring is primarily valuable for senior executives who have already risen through the ranks of individual contribution and middle management (though that journey can happen surprisingly fast in startup environments), and is an alternative to the default style of working 1:1 with executives, which is generally called *coaching*. Unlike in sports, the two are hard to combine for reasons I'll get to.

A question I've wondered about over the years is: can sparring skills be taught, assuming a broadly suitable temperament and an aptitude for it? I've been at it for over a decade, and it probably took me three years to get it to consistently good enough that I felt I could do it with almost anybody. Can that learning curve be shortened? Yes and no.

Some aspects of the skill acquisition can be speeded up. Some things that took me years to figure out, I can probably teach in a day or two. But other elements of getting ready for the role—like reading widely and deeply about technology and business to develop an appreciative worldview of it (a sparring *Weltanschauung* if you will) took me decades (I've been reading business and technology books since I was a teenager), and I don't think can be speeded up. I think it will take *anyone* decades.

Fortunately, if you're interested in developing sparring skills at all, you've probably already been doing the right kind of preparation anyway for other reasons, including plain curiosity. So you're probably more prepared than you realize. It's a question of recognizing the significance of what you've been doing, *wax-on-wax-off* style, as in the *Karate Kid* movies. But you're probably not as prepared as you need to be.

In the pilot workshop, I finally got a chance to try and explain and demonstrate the model to a small group of six willing guinea pigs. The participants were six indie consultants like myself, most of whom already had significant experience working with senior executives in a similar mode, but wanted to refine their practice and understanding of it, and make it more legible to themselves, to be able to continuously improve their practice.

In these final four chapters of Volume 1, I will be covering the core ideas of sparring. My goal is to both explain the model to

those who want to try it, and to provide a detailed example of the
sort of foundational consulting idea that can sustain an indie-
consulting practice. In this introductory part, I want to do three
things:

1. define sparring
2. distinguish it from other 1:1 relational practices like
   coaching
3. situate it in the broader context of executive
   development

In the rest of this series, I will work through how to actually
develop sparring-partner skills, and a consulting business based on
those skills.

SPARRING AS LIVE THEORIZING

The goal of sparring is simple: *to improve the quality of live theorizing
executives do around their ongoing work.*

The central insight driving the practice of sparring is that busy
executives typically do not have time to do more than dip into fully
formed theories of management or leadership, delivered through
books, or executive education. Even the case method MBA students
learn, which rests on live conversation/debate in groups, is too far
removed from actual live situations to serve the purpose.

If you've ever read an HBR case study, you've probably had that
uncanny sensation of looking at the business problem-solving
equivalent of stock photography. A lot of fresh MBAs, who earned
their degree perhaps too early, come across that way to me when
they talk. They come across as smart, prepared, and with interesting things to say, but fundamentally lacking in serious exposure
to live-fire, high-stakes executive decision-making.

For strong executives, theorizing happens in a rough-and-ready
form in the context of live action, working out how to act in, or

respond to, specific situations unfolding *now*, involving *specific* people, constraints, and timelines.

Weak executives, by contrast, often come across as eager to avoid, sidestep, or ignore the hardest parts of the situations they are being paid the big bucks to handle. Much of their thinking happens on the sidelines, around situations that *might* unfold. Often their theorizing is *too* polished and refined—a dead giveaway that they're far from the live-fire action.

Consider the analogous situation in boxing. Top boxers might study videos of an opponent for an upcoming title fight with their trainer, form a hypothesis about their weaknesses, and workshop bout strategies *for that specific upcoming bout* with a sparring partner. For example, Muhammad Ali famously did exactly that in preparing for his Rumble in the Jungle bout against George Foreman, abandoning the "float like a butterfly, sting like a bee" style he was famous for, and adopting a "rope-a-dope" style designed to wear out Foreman. Wikipedia describes how that came about:

> According to photographer George Kalinsky, Ali had an unusual way of conducting his sparring sessions, where he had his sparring partner hit him, which he felt "was his way of being able to take punishment in the belly." Kalinsky told him: "Do what you do in a training session: Act like a dope on the ropes." Ali then replied: "So, you want me to be a rope-a-dope?"
>
> According to Angelo Dundee, Kalinsky told Ali: "Why don't you try something like that? Sort of a dope on the ropes, letting Foreman swing away but, like in the picture, hit nothing but air." The publicist John Condon popularized the phrase "rope-a-dope."

If this anecdote is accurate, then Ali's intellectual sparring partner, as opposed to the one in the ring, was the photographer Kalinsky. It's weird how often it ends up working like this. You might talk for hours, but in the end, it's one casual phrase or thought that ends up unlocking the critical idea. My very first client said as much to me—that after twenty hours of chatting, the value I delivered all down to one phrase I happened to drop casually in thinking through a problem: "penny auction." Two seconds in twenty hours. That pattern has repeated for nine years. Hours and hours of conversation and emails, punctuated by scattered moments of high-leverage usable insight—a phrase here, a 2x2 there, a particular quote or metaphor that fits the situation. It used to frustrate me a lot initially. Was there no way to cut out all the hours and formulaically arrive at just those moments of insight? So far I haven't found one. You have to put in the time—and learn to enjoy it.

Insights like this cannot be found in textbooks, cranked out of fully-formed theories, or by "solving" cartoon case studies in a classroom setting (the equivalent of a punching bag or boxing dummy). They can only emerge through the process of preparing mindfully for specific live-fire challenges with a live sparring partner who can keep up with you.

Like good boxers, good executives instinctively seem to follow a similar, highly situational preparation regimen. They typically study developing situations that require action (many even like the "review the game tape" metaphor), form one or more working hypotheses about how to tackle them, and workshop them with trusted partners before actually trying them live. At any given time, they are shepherding a dozen situations along towards resolution, and workshopping multiple ideas about what to do, often with multiple sparring partners. This short passage from a classic paper by Karl Weick, *What Theory is Not, Theorizing Is*,[1] gets at the essence:

> Products of the theorizing process seldom emerge as full-blown theories, which means that most of what passes for theory in organizational studies consists of approximations. Although these approximations vary in their generality, few of them take the form of strong theory, and most of them can be read as texts created "in lieu of" strong theories. These substitutes for theory may result

from lazy theorizing in which people try to graft theory onto stark sets of data. But they may also represent interim struggles in which people intentionally inch towards stronger theories. *The products of laziness and intense struggles may look the same and consist of references, data, lists, diagrams, and hypotheses.* To label these five as "not theory" makes sense if the problem is laziness and incompetence. But ruling out those same five may slow inquiry if the problem is theoretical development still in its early stages. *[emphasis added]*

I quote this passage on my own consulting website and describe sparring in relation to it as follows:

The bulk of my practice comprises 1:1 work with senior executives as a conversational sparring partner, *to stress test and improve the rigor and quality of their ongoing thinking about their evolving challenges.*

Of course, executive work is not boxing. Meeting rooms are not boxing rings (though they can sometimes feel that way). Purposes in organizations are generally more aligned, non-zero-sum, and non-adversarial than in a boxing ring. The preparation is much more of an intellectual process. But many of the challenges of preparation are very similar.

WHO CAN SPAR?

The executive sparring partner role is a relatively new kind of external consulting role for a simple reason—the kind of immersive shared context required between client and sparring partner could not exist 30 years ago, due to the sheer difficulty of creating the shared knowledge environment in pre-digital environments. This means, historically, the role has almost always been played by trusted insiders and colleagues rather than paid outsiders. Usually, executives spar with trusted peers who understand the industry well enough to keep up. Common sparring partners include:

1. an executive in another company in an adjacent non-competing business
2. a board member, key investor, or a retired executive from the same organization
3. an academic studying the industry or domain (rare)
4. A peer executive in the same company

That last option is less common than you'd expect. Conflicts of interest often prevent direct peers from serving as sparring partners for each other, despite being the best suited for it in other ways. Peer executives are often competing with each other for power, influence, and control over specific situations, so mutual sparring support is limited to windows of opportunity when they are *not* striving at cross-purposes.

Despite these problems, peer-to-peer sparring still constitutes the vast bulk of sparring going on in the world, simply because of the numbers involved. It is just a highly unpredictable and unreliable source of sparring support. If an executive relies solely on peers for sparring support, they may find it unavailable just when they most need it. Basically, it is surprisingly hard for senior executives to find the combination of three key required traits in *one* reliably available person:

1. sufficient domain knowledge to allow shared thinking in insider-language
2. absence of conflicts of interest and misalignments that get in the way of trust
3. intellectual capacity to process at the typically demanding level

In the past, these three requirements often ended up creating a pick-2-of-3 triangle in a field comprising only insider candidates. Outsiders typically faced far too many barriers acquiring enough domain knowledge to play the role. Until the internet happened.

THE INTERNET AS SPARRING ARENA

Thanks to the internet, it is possible for vast numbers of people who are technically outsiders to keep up with an industry or a specific company from the outside, participate in lively discourses around it, and be generally informed and prepared enough to play sparring-partner roles.

Today, often all it takes to form a surprisingly deep and useful mental model of an organization is a few hours spent on Google, LinkedIn, Glassdoor, Wikipedia, and social media. Throw in a phone call or email or two, and you are probably 80% of the way there, even before signing an NDA and being given a peek at internal information.

And you do not need expensive subscriptions to business intelligence or dossier services to do so. Most of the valuable situation awareness information is free.

Add to that the trend towards increasing openness—many executives openly discussing their challenges on Twitter among other things—and the set of potential sparring partners available to any executive vastly expand. In fact, many seem to show up on Twitter to do exactly that—free sparring sessions with random members of the public!

If you're an executive at a small, cash-starved startup and cannot afford to pay for a sparring partner, I highly recommend this approach. To the extent you can, just blog or tweet publicly about your work, and you're very likely to find the sparring you need for free.

And if you're looking to get into the business of being a sparring partner, there's no better training ground than Twitter. You can literally provoke and engage thousands of executives. You're very likely to get your first clients that way. I got my first couple of clients via Quora, and almost all the rest through some social media outlet or the other—Twitter, my own blog, contributions to industry blogs, and so on.

But information availability, while necessary, is not sufficient. Being a sparring partner calls for a particular temperament and personality (not learnable), and a particular mode of being attuned to others (learnable).

SPARRING PARTNER AS AN ARCHETYPE

I've previously written about the idea of consultants as a well-defined archetype—Jungian shadows. This is particularly true of sparring partners. In *Elements of Consulting Style*, I introduced a 2x2 of four types of 1:1 consulting roles, corresponding to four types of clients: achiever, integrator, tester, explorer. While most clients are a mix of the four types, most consultants, in my experience, can typically only serve only one of these roles well.

Let's get at the elements of the sparring partner archetype (both innate and learnable) via comparisons with the other three.

Unlike a *therapist or life coach*, a sparring partner does *not* support inner work except occasionally as a side effect. Psychological insight into human nature is helpful, but not central to effective sparring.

Unlike *philosophical counselors or mentors*, the sparring partner does *not* occupy the position of a respected elder guiding an executive through inner or outer challenges they themselves have already been through. Your own banked growth experiences are helpful, but not central, to effective sparring.

Unlike an *executive coach or teacher*, the sparring partner does *not* support general-purpose behavioral development (forming good habits, losing bad ones, developing specific skills), in areas like productivity, emotional self-regulation, or "crucial conversations." Behavioral insight is helpful, but not central.

What *is* central to effective sparring partnerships is actual understanding of the business domain and organizational environment. Having access to the enabling background knowledge is one half of the problem—largely solved by the internet. But actually being able to *think on your feet* with that knowledge is a different matter altogether, and the other half of the problem—one most people will fail at.

Often, this is a matter of the sparring partner having enough relevant career experience. People in classic "coaching" roles usually do not—they often have backgrounds in helping professions/fields like psychology, social work, or HR, but rarely in the fields where executives tend to emerge.

Most executives typically have career backgrounds (if not educational) in technology, finance, sales, or marketing, and are facing deep problems in those functional line-management domains. They usually need sparring partners who have at least a passing familiarity with the domains their work touches.

CEOs typically face problems that transcend even those functional domain boundaries and require knowledge going beyond, in that nebulous pile of backstopping activity that is "leadership." They require sparring partners with domain/function experience *and* something more—a philosophical fit of sparring styles. These requirements make casting for sparring roles much harder than for coaching roles. It's not a problem that can be solved by credentialing.

Executives typically know they're *not* looking for traditional executive coaching, but can't quite put a finger on what they *are* looking for. But they can recognize it when they see it.

CASTING FOR SPARRING

Executives seeking sparring support often unconsciously look for sparring partners they can talk to in their own language, without having to constantly explain themselves, dumb themselves down, or having to provide quick tutorials on basic working concepts at every conversational turn. They might provide a few pointers to learning resources, if they *really* want to work with you, but even that is rare. In general, they will expect you to know enough to spar with them effectively in the very first hour. As a rule of thumb, if an executive has to spend more than half the time in the first hour of a sparring engagement explaining basic background ideas (especially basic technical concepts or basic business ideas like how to read a balance sheet), it's not going to work out.

The ideal sparring partner is someone who already has a sense of the history of the industry and its technological foundations, has some functional depth in all the important domains the executive has to deal with, and has already been thinking about the latest fads doing the rounds.

The ideal sparring partner already has an opinionated take on important questions that are at least wrong (rather than not-even-wrong, which is the most common state), based on having kept up with the industry in question.

How do I know this? I know this because my clients have disproportionately been technology leaders, either leading technology/engineering functions, or having risen to CEO-level general roles from the technology leadership side. And this is not an accident. It is because I'm an engineer by training myself, and much of my writing and social media presence is suffused with technology references, metaphors, analogies, and historical anecdotes.

For a technology leader who reads one of my blog posts or a Twitter thread, it is immediately obvious that it won't take me painfully long to get sufficiently up to speed to serve as a useful sparring partner. I'm not going to be asking a machine learning company CEO what an eigenvalue is. I am not going to be terminally befuddled by a chemical industry CEO mentioning the ring structure of benzene. Or by a CFO talking about gross margins and EBIDTA.

I'll say more about this knowledge preparedness aspect later in this series, but make no mistake—sparring is a knowledge-intensive role. You have to know a lot, and showcase what you know, just to get in the game. And you have to be willing to learn a lot, very rapidly and efficiently, at short notice, to stay in the game.

If you have the temperament, you'll already know it. You probably read widely outside your field, and fairly deeply. You keep up with industry-level trends in one or more large sectors at a play-by-play level. You keep up with science and technology news at more than a casual level. You can parse at least half of any casual insider conversation you might hear about any industry in a coffee shop, and three-quarters if you're given a few minutes to google stuff.

You don't get there overnight of course. It takes years of being interested in business and technology and keeping up. But fortunately, it's not a specialized kind of interest or attention. Whatever your reasons for your past interest and curiosity in business and technology, the fruits are going to be valuable in a sparring role.

SPARRING IN EXECUTIVE DEVELOPMENT

Let me wrap up this looong first part by placing sparring partners in the context of executive development more broadly. The short version is this: there is no element of sparring anywhere in the typical executive development offering suite, which is why I have an indie career at all.

The traditional executive coaching model does not work for sparring, because most coaches do not have the right background to serve as sparring partners. Other elements of the leadership development world do not address the need either. People in that world do acknowledge the need, but generally leave it alone as an area to be covered by mutual peer-to-peer support. Which also does not work great for reasons I've already pointed out.

The slightly longer version. Back in 2008, when I was still confused enough about my own life priorities to imagine I might want to be on the executive-suite track myself, I was sent off by my employer, Xerox, to an "early high potential" leadership retreat at the Center for Creative Leadership, where I was subjected to a battery of psychological tests (Myers-Briggs, FIRO-

B, CPI 260, Skillscope 360 . . .). See this pile of material I came home with.

| Creative leadership testing flotsam

It was all a lot of fun, but felt like a bit of a LARP. Like I was pretending to be someone I was not—and doing it fairly well. Clearly, in some way I fit into this world, but not the way I was present in it during that program. The capstone piece of the retreat was a couple of sessions with an executive coach. It was the first time I had done anything like it, and my expectations were low.

The exposure to executive coaching was particularly valuable because the coach assigned to me was pretty good at it, and it was a valuable session as a *coaching* session. I came away impressed by how well the coach had been able to get under my skin, and help me see some things about my behaviors. But I also came away with the impression that useful though it was, it somehow wasn't even remotely helpful in relation to the actual challenges I was facing at the time, in leading my project teams.

Perhaps that was just a matter of finding the right coach? Unfortunately, that's not the case. I learned that my experience of coaching was in fact typical from a book I read around that time:

What Got You Here, Won't Get You There, by Marshall Goldsmith, a pioneering executive coach, who in some ways invented the field.

Goldsmith is known for pioneering the modern style of executive coaching, focused on behavioral rough edges. It begins with the assumption that anyone headed for the executive suite already has high competence and capability in their core leadership/managerial areas, but might require help addressing one or more seemingly innocuous blindspots and behavioral rough spots that end up being a huge liability.

Goldsmith's model is the mainstay of 1:1 coaching models. As far as I can tell, all executive coaches practice some version of it, even if they're not aware of it. Unfortunately, the Goldsmith model has its limitations, and it became clear to me that coaching was not going to be the source of the kind of support I could actually use. Though I didn't know it then, and didn't call it that, what I needed —and never got—was sparring support. The few people around capable of serving in a sparring partner role with me were far too busy to spare more than the occasional hour, and usually available only when they wanted to talk to me, not when I wanted to talk to them.

Cut to three years later, in 2011, with my first couple of clients, it immediately became clear that what I was doing was in fact sparring—filling the gap I had myself perceived from the other side in 2008. The idea that sparring is a distinct kind of 1:1 relational work has since been repeatedly validated by my experiences. In fact, several of my wealthier clients have hired me for sparring while *already* working with both a coach and a therapist. These have been some of my best sparring relationships because the client already recognizes that these are different support roles that call for different sorts of people to be cast in them. The sparring work does not accidentally slide into these adjacent kinds of work that I have neither the temperament nor the taste for.

That's it for my introduction to sparring. In the coming chapters I cover several other topics: how to prepare for a sparring role, how to conduct yourself in a sparring session and in the follow through, assessing fit with a potential client, what kinds of potential clients to seek out or avoid, scoping engagements and setting expectations correctly, and how to find interesting sparring roles.

---

1. *Administrative Science Quarterly*, 1995 www.jstor.org/stable/2393789

30

THE GURU FACTOR

THE PERILS AND PERKS OF A PRECEPTOR POSTURE

IN THE PREVIOUS CHAPTER, I introduced the idea of executive sparring as a practice distinct from coaching. Continuing the series, in this chapter I want to talk about the most crucial aspect of being a sparring partner—developing and embodying a deep, appreciative worldview complementary to that of leaders of organizations, which makes you a useful foil to them in their work.

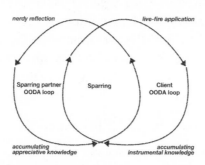

| Sparring OODA loops

For better or worse, getting into the sparring partner business means coming to terms with a growing perception of a guru factor around what you do—*even if you are younger and less experienced than your clients.* This is a fraught business. It creates serious reputational jeopardy. There is a fine line between *business guru* and *laughing stock* (or to use a more appropriate modern term, *lolcow*).

The jeopardy turns into double jeopardy if you happen to be Indian. And into triple jeopardy if your middle name happens to literally be *Guru*. I'm not complaining. Just noting obvious facts.

So a good way to start figuring out the core of the appreciative worldview that can potentially form the core of your sparring practice is to own the guru-jeopardy and ask—*what am I a guru of?*

Take a stab at answering that question before we unpack the concept. As a hint: contemporary Western usages such as *Unix guru, design guru,* and of course, *management guru,* are actually closer to what I think is the correct understanding of *gurudom* than the literal translation of *teacher.* The core of gurudom is not a teacher-student relationship, but a seeker-world relationship.

Nerding out over the innards of Unix, and developing an appreciative worldview through the lens of that nerding out, is closer to the true spirit of gurudom than being good at teaching computing skills. Gurudom is nerddom *plus a certain guru factor.*

Being a computer science teacher makes you a good person to learn (say) sorting algorithms or good Python style from. But being a Unix guru makes you fun to *spar* with about the future of computing, and an interesting companion for explorations of that future. People can go as deep as they like with you, knowing that you can keep up, even if you don't agree with them.

SPARRING AND APPRECIATIVE KNOWLEDGE

Appreciative worldviews, which are at the heart of guru factors, emerge via accumulation of *appreciative knowledge,* a term due to urbanist John Friedman, who defines it in his book *Planning in the Public Domain*[1] as follows:

The social validation of knowledge through mastery of the world puts the stress on *manipulative* knowledge. But knowledge can also serve another purpose, which is the construction of satisfying images of the world. Such knowledge, which is pursued primarily for the worldview that it opens up, may be called *appreciative* knowledge. Contemplation and creation of symbolic forms continue to be pursued as ways of knowing about the world, but because they are not immediately useful, they are not validated socially, and are treated as merely private concerns or entertainment.

Friedman uses the term *manipulative knowledge* in opposition to *appreciative*, but he doesn't mean manipulative in a Machiavellian sense. He simply means knowledge of how to actually do things to drive change in the world, accumulated by actually trying to do those things.[2] In this post I want to apply the distinction to consulting work, especially sparring.

Here is the big idea to keep in mind: *About 90% of your effectiveness as a sparring partner derives from the depth of your appreciative worldview, developed and expressed through critical reading, writing, podcasts, and talks. Only about 10% depends on your in-session sparring skills.* In this, sparring skill is similar to negotiation skill. In negotiations, 90% of success depends on the preparation you do *before* you sit down at the negotiation table. Only about 10% depends on your negotiation skill.

GURUS *VS.* PUNDITS

These activities at the core of strengthening appreciative capacity—reading, writing, podcasts, and talks—are not primarily marketing activities, though they do serve a marketing function as a side-effect. They are integral to developing your capacity for sparring, but pursuing them for the *sake* of getting better at sparring doesn't work.

I think of these activities as *nerdy reflection*, something very few people have much time for. It's a time-wasting, bunny-trail-exploring nerding-out over the significance of things you're seeing in your life.

So how do you develop appreciative capacity? The linked OODA-loops[3] diagram at the beginning of this chapter should convey the gist. You and the client are each driving complementary OODA loops that intersect in the practice of sparring. You are inside each other's OODA loops in a way that mutually reinforces *both* your learning processes. Yours is an appreciative learning process, theirs is an instrumental learning process. This means you cannot become a "guru" at something by deciding to study all the classics relevant to your interests. That turns you into an erudite scholar, an entirely different thing.

Why? For much the same reason you cannot become a Unix guru by reading scholarly papers and books about operating systems. You have to be at the keyboard, messing around with shell scripts, hacking away. More generally, you cannot develop appreciative capacities in instrumental ways, any more than you can develop instrumental capacities in appreciative ways.

Here is another way to think about it: you cannot learn how to swim by reading a hydrodynamics textbook on dry land. But equally, you cannot figure out the molecular structure and chemical properties of water simply by swimming around in it. This distinction is easy to get when we're talking about swimming *vs.* chemistry, but gets a little tricky and very meta when we are talking about instrumental *vs.* appreciative approaches to *book-learning itself*.

The thing is, instrumental behaviors develop prowess at instrumental capabilities rather than appreciative capacities, *even when the object of the learning activity is appreciative knowledge*. You *do* have to develop your instrumental scholarship capacities to some degree, but they can't be the primary focus. That is not to say becoming an erudite scholar with a command over the canonical texts of a tradition is not a worthwhile thing. Go for it if that's your thing. It just doesn't develop sparring capacity or a guru factor.

If you are a completist about Sanskrit words for these things, the word for erudite scholarship has been imported into English as well: *pundit*.[4] The differences are worth noting:

- Pundits engage in scholarly debate with each other within an institutional tradition and are governed by conventions and hierarchies. Gurus spar with all interesting comers, be they beggars or princes, and in any context.

- Pundits can become institutional stewards of traditions, but rarely create new traditions. Gurus often create new traditions, but usually end up on the margins of even traditions they helped create.

- Pundits often gain a great deal of worldly fame, wealth, and power, and this is viewed as just reward for their institution-building work. Gurus on the other hand, rarely do, and if they do, are viewed as having sullied their reputations.

- Pundits represent and embody institutional epistemic authority and take offense at challenges to that authority. Gurus have no such formal *locus standi* in relation to the traditions they may draw upon, and are rarely offended by challenges to their authority because they claim none to begin with.

- Pundits often participate in visibly ceremonial and ritual forms of knowledge performance as the core of their work (traditionally, conducting temple services or sacrificial rites). Gurus typically do not. In consulting, this maps to doing talks or workshops around fully formed theories, *vs.* informal theorizing discourses.

- Pundits often present in highly ceremonial and authoritative ways, with a strong and consciously crafted halo,[5] but often accompanied by ritual protestations of humility. Gurus stereotypically present in self-effacing ways, often being mistaken for beggars, but also often present in poorly socialized ways, as irritable curmudgeons or unpredictable trolls for example.

- Pundits typically enjoy teaching, usually do it very well, and seek out opportunities to do more of it. Gurus typically don't enjoy teaching, usually do it poorly, and seek excuses to avoid doing it.

The tension between pundits and gurus is so commonplace, it is practically a trope in Indian history. Similar archetype pairs exist in other traditions. In the Christian tradition, the distinction between regular and secular clergy is somewhat similar, as is the one between research and teaching faculties in universities. A loosely similar modern pair is the Straussian distinction[6] between *great thinkers* and *scholars*, though that one is fraught with additional political-philosophical baggage and conservative norms of reverence of ancient traditions that makes it not quite analogous. Why does all this matter? It matters because *appreciative knowledge is not punditry.* Punditry *is the result of an instrumental approach to appreciative knowledge.* Gurudom *by contrast, is the result of an appreciative approach to instrumental knowledge.*[7]

In the world of consulting, gurus favor free-form sparring, backroom influence, and proximity to consequential decision-making. Pundits favor developing and delivering workshops and talks, building scaled institutions, and crafting powerful public images. Pundits develop personal brands (if not always strong ones). Gurus develop reputations (if not always flattering ones). Both usually do at least a little of the other kind of activity out of necessity, but basically you have to choose and choose fairly early which path to go down. It's like figuring out if you're left-handed or right-handed. I've done my share of workshops, public speaking, and teaching. But none of that stuff comes naturally to me, I'm not very good at it, and I don't enjoy it much. For better or worse, I've wandered down the guru path rather than the pundit path.

PERIPHERAL LEARNING

What do I mean by *appreciative approach to instrumental knowledge*? A good way to think of it is: Gurudom is weakly codified appreciative knowledge of the sort that develops on the peripheries of instrumental practice. The kind of knowledge that develops when you let attention wander towards the margins of instrumental activity, to metacognitive musings around it. You do have to *play*, but if playing well becomes the whole point, you're better suited to playing excellence than coaching excellence.

Here we run into a problem though. Letting your attention wander to the margins of instrumental activity is *dangerous*. If you do it in mission-critical situations, you can become distracted and make costly errors. This is one reason the best sports coaches often turn to coaching after mediocre careers as players. A weakness for metacognitive distraction that diminishes performance on the field turns into a strength in coaching.

In live-fire situations, letting your mind wander to metacognitive concerns is often a sign of an even deeper weakness. It is a displacement activity triggered by fear or anxiety, rather than actual philosophical curiosity about meta-concerns. This sort of person does *not* turn into a good coach, because they typically exit the live game with too much insecurity to serve as effective foils to better players. There is, however, one activity which allows you to safely let a significant portion of your attention wander to the margins of instrumental activity. This is of course sparring.

LINKED LEARNING LOOPS

We are now in a position to appreciate the linked-loops diagram representing the sparring process that we started this chapter with.

Sparring is a safe-fail activity immediately adjacent to live-fire activity. It benefits from a little bit of peripheral attention-wandering. It benefits from the kind of experimental trial-and-error attitude, accompanied by mindful critical attention, that is fueled by things you notice out of the corner of your eye. Appreciative knowledge developed through the work of peripheral attention during sparring is what compounds gurudom and makes you better able to spar.

This might sound like "the best way to get good at sparring is to do more sparring," but that's not quite it. While there is a component of mindful deliberate practice, it is only necessary, not sufficient, and it's not unique to the sparring *partner.* The principal too, has to be mindful in that exact same way during sparring sessions, letting attention go to peripheral vision to a far greater extent than they would in the ring during an actual bout.

What makes the sparring *partner* role different is that you take the fruits of marginal attention around sparring and convert them into *nerdy explorations* which then turn into fodder for your own private pursuit of things that interest you (via writing, reading, and such), creating a growing store of *appreciative knowledge*. It is a virtuous cycle that powers growing gurudom. This is the left-side loop in the diagram.

The yang to that yin is the loop experienced by the client you are sparring with. In the best case, the same sparring experience is cashed out differently. For the client, the fruits of marginal attention around sparring are converted into superior *live-fire application*, which leads to a growing store of *instrumental knowledge*. This is the right-side loop in the diagram.

These two loops—both of which are metacognitive OODA loops with the sparring serving as an *orientation* activity for *both* parties—are at the heart of sparring. Where this beautiful symmetry breaks down is in the relative value of the two loops. The client's loop passes through the real world. The sparring partner's loop passes through the adjacent-possible band of the real world. The former, by virtue of having more skin in the game, is worth much more money. This is why the client typically pays the sparring partner rather than the other way around.

If the sparring sessions go well, the client will be forged into a better live-fire decision-maker and leader, while you will develop tendencies of a guru-like nature, whether or not you want them.

RECOGNIZING GURUDOM

The process I've described above should make it clear that you cannot actually *choose* to become a guru. Equally if you're doing certain things well enough to be paid to continue doing them, you cannot *avoid* becoming a guru either. This means gurudom is a tendency in your life that you *recognize* and come to terms with at some point, based on how people are choosing to relate to you. Including both how they are laughing or sneering at you, and how they are praising and appreciating you. Again, think *Unix guru, design guru,* or *management guru.* Not *guy with long beard running a commune, with sex slaves in the basement, and Rolls Royces in the garage.* Some willingly lean into gurudom, some have it thrust at them.[8]

Gurudom is *not* primarily about a teacher-student relationship. A guru or equivalent concept in other cultures is rarely primarily a teacher, though teaching activity usually occurs on the margins of gurudom. The concept of a guru combines four elements that all play a role in sparring:

1. reluctant teaching that is closer to preceptorship
2. individual striving for esoteric appreciative knowledge
3. the capacity to keep up with others on *their* journeys
4. a degree of genuine (and costly) indifference to worldly rewards

Of the four, the teaching element in a conventional sense is the *least* important. It is the one that can be most easily delegated to others, and often is, at the first opportunity.

In the traditional Indian education model, known as the *guru-shishya parampara* (literally, "teacher-student tradition"), only the very earliest stages—the first few years—look like conventional teaching, focused on drills, repetition, and homework. And these are often handled by senior students of the guru, just as graduate students do much of the actual teaching in American universities.

Teaching responsibilities can in fact seriously interfere with the actual responsibilities of gurudom, which are closer to "research" in the academic sense, but not quite the same. As a result, gurudom finds its best expression via two core activities: sparring with peers in the same intellectual weight class, and through the ongoing development of an appreciative worldview. This latter activity can be understood as being a preceptor, which is closely adjacent to, but not the same as, being a teacher.

The natural fit with sparring and preceptorship is why faculty in American research universities are generally terrible teachers, prefer Ph.D. students to undergraduates, and prefer to treat those Ph.D. students as much as peers as possible, often handling actual advising responsibilities with great reluctance.

As with universities, which evolved in the West from the priest-hood, with its vows of poverty and chastity, the guru tradition too has an uncomfortable relationship with worldly wealth. In India, gurus were traditionally expected to live in simplicity and relative poverty in humble *ashrams* in the forest, outside the civilizational core. They were expected to spar with kings, train princes, groom their own replacements, and produce pundits for the institutions that needed them. The word is usually translated as *hermitage* in English, but modern-day *ashrams* run by literal gurus are often relatively luxurious retreat destinations, suitable for entertaining kings and presidents, with great comfort lurking beneath a facade of theatrical simplicity.

Management gurus of course, usually skip the simplicity

signaling and go straight for the 5-star leadership retreat experience in lieu of real ashrams. The spirit of the *ashram* tradition is
today best represented by the research laboratory, rather than a
luxurious leadership retreat campus.

EMISSARY OF THE ADJACENT POSSIBLE

Past the basic drilling stages, in the traditional Indian model the
student progresses to something that resembles more of a sparring
process, focused on debates and disputations around classic texts.
These start out as rehearsals of traditional arguments around age-
old questions, heavy with appeals to authority, and progress to
increasingly free-form open debates on the live questions of the
day. By the time the student gets to advanced stages, striving to best
the master is the expected mode of engagement.

Here a fork in the road appears. The princes, of course, go back
to their kingdoms, assassinate their fathers, and ascend to their
thrones. As adults, they may return to spar with their gurus. As for
the rest, some head towards punditry—stewards of the tradition
within institutions embedded in secular life within the civilizational core. Others stay on the margins and head towards gurudom
in their own right—setting up the equivalent of experimental labo-
ratories for their own nerdy reflections as best as they can.

This developmental path is not restricted to intellectual traditions. You can see a similar path in Indian music education, which
begins, as in the West, with young students practicing scales and set
compositions in *ragas,* and moves on to learning to render compositions in particular styles, peculiar to specific traditions. But at this
point it diverges from the Western music tradition, and heads
towards the free-form structured improvisation that is *raga* performance. These performances often involve a strong element of sparring with accompanying musicians (similar to call-and-response
jamming as in jazz) known as *jugalbandi.* Versions of this can be
found all over the world of course. In Japanese martial arts for

instance, we find the idea of *kihon* (drills), *kata* (set forms), and *kumite* (sparring). In the medieval European tradition of gallantry, noble-born boys were sent off to serve as squires to peer knights where they learned jousting, horsemanship, and other knightly skills. Historically, this kind of education has always been something of a luxury, since it cannot be delivered at scale. Around the world, it was largely only available to princes being groomed for imperial leadership roles, or commoner students showing some promise as future pundits and gurus. There is a reason it is generally restricted to business executives today—paying someone in your intellectual weight class to spar 1:1 with you is not cheap.

For those providing this kind of education, the core activity—call it research, call it nerdy reflection, call it saddling senior students with the real teaching duties and sneaking off down bunny trails—became a way of life. Those who adopted this way of life, whether they were called gurus or something else, primarily engaged with the civilizational core by sparring with its leaders—and those being groomed for leadership—at the margins.

That is the essence of the guru factor—your stake in the margins of civilization, as an embodiment and emissary of the adjacent possible, bringing appreciative knowledge to life in the real world.

That's a rather nebulous thing to try and be. But the core is simple enough—spar, nerd-out, write/speak about, spar some more. Pick people who you can keep up with, and who can keep up with you, as your sparring counter parties, *regardless of what they can pay you.* Recognize the adjacent activity of punditry and consciously choose one or the other.

The rest is just a matter of doing this steadily, for years, making money as best you can along the way.

<hr>

To conclude this peek at gurudom, consider a key diagnostic question: *what are you a guru of?*

Gurudom is something that creeps up on you after years of messing around, nerding out over things that interest you, and sparring with people. If you do have an answer, it is probably something that happened when you weren't really looking. For me, it happened to be organizational sociopathy and office politics.

The good news is, if you're a guru of something, it isn't a box that contains and confines you. That's a price you pay for the rewards of punditry. To be a guru of something is to look at the world *through* that thing rather than being put in a box *defined* by that thing. There are no restrictions on what you're allowed to look at. The thing you're a guru of is merely the appreciative perspective on the world people associate with you. In other words, if people want to learn *about* X, they go looking for a pundit of X. If they want to see some aspect of the world *through* X, they go looking for a guru of X.

You can now ask useful follow-up questions to further understand who you are:

- Is your relationship to appreciative knowledge closer to punditry or gurudom?
- Is that what you actually want?
- If you somehow ended up on the wrong side of that divide relative to your natural inclinations, how do you cross over?
- How should you relate to those on the other side? As complements? Evil twins? Deadly rivals?

---

1. www.amazon.com/dp/0691022682
2. I prefer the term *instrumental knowledge* for this.
3. OODA stands for *Observer-Orient-Decide-Act*. The OODA loop is the core diagram of a decision-making philosophy developed by Col. John Boyd in the 1970s, and is commonly used in business and military settings today. A good reference for it is Chet Richards' *Certain to Win*. Volume 2 contains a section on applying OODA thinking to indie consulting life. The diagram in this chapter is a pair of stylized, interlocking OODA loops.

4. In India it is usually spelled *Pandit* and is a common last name, as is Acharya which is roughly synonymous.

5. See *What Color is Your Halo?* earlier in this volume.

6. "Straussian" is an adjective commonly applied to a style of discourse associated with the political philosopher Leo Strauss.

7. For completeness of the 2x2, an appreciative approach to appreciative knowledge makes you a critic and an instrumental approach to instrumental knowledge makes you a vocational learner.

8. And some, like me, have it hang over their entire lives thanks to nominative determinism—I've been the butt of "guru" jokes since age 10, thanks to my middle name.

31

THE SPARRING ARENA

SETTING UP THE PROBLEM SOCIAL GRAPH IN SPARRING

IN THE PREVIOUS chapter I teed up a deeper dive into the sorts of appreciative knowledge that prepare you for sparring. In this chapter, I want to tackle the assumptions you must make about yourself, the client, and other people to construct what I call the *problem social graph,* which is the foundation of sparring. This is the configuration of other players in the organizational context relevant to the problems the client is trying to solve through sparring. This context is in some sense the sparring arena. Here's the core idea:

> In sparring the best starting assumption to adopt is *I'm okay, you're okay, they're not so hot.*

I'm going to call this the *Central Dogma of Sparring,* and there's an illustration of the concept on the next page. The reference, for those of you unfamiliar with it, is to the 1967 transactional analysis pop classic, *I'm Ok, You're Ok,* which inspired a parody titled *I'm Ok, You're Not So Hot.* This starting assumption might seem unreasonably gloomy and in fact goes against some very good management wisdom. Douglas McGregor's Theory X vs. Theory Y, for example,

suggests that the best assumption to make about others in an organization is that they're actually competent and good by default.

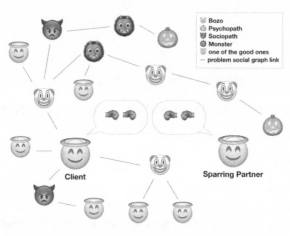

| *Central Dogma of Sparring*

The essence of the sparring assumption is that the client is not
the problem, and neither are you, the sparring partner. The
problem is other people. This is *not* in general a good assumption
to make about situations or organizations. So why is it a good
assumption to make about sparring relationship setups?

First, they are seeking out a sparring partner because they have
real problems they want to work through. It takes being fairly
severely stymied for someone to seek out a sparring partner, so the
problem is likely real.

Second, they are seeking out a *sparring* partner rather than a
mentor, therapist, or functional/domain expert, which means they
are preparing for conflict, which usually means they see *specific
other people* as the problem rather than say a technical challenge or
information ambiguity.

Third, though humans are of course prone to primary attribu-
tion error (blaming individual traits instead of situational factors
for others' behaviors), if you're sparring with an experienced senior

manager or executive, chances are they're good judges of character and experienced at sorting out people vs. situational factors. Otherwise they wouldn't be where they are.

Fourth, though people *in general* tend to adopt lazy habits when it comes to psychology, convincing themselves that others are the problem so they don't have to change, this is usually not as much of a factor with the sorts of ambitious people who end up as executives.

In my case, there is a fifth factor. As someone whose reputation was initially established on the basis of rather bleak writings about sociopathic office politics (many of my leads come from writings like *The Gervais Principle, Be Slightly Evil,* and *Entrepreneurs are the New Labor*), there is a further selection effect, where people seek me out specifically for those kinds of problems.

I suspect this generalizes too. Those who write with more positive frames are likely to attract engagements that are not structured as sparring engagements. So if you get into sparring at all, chances are there is a streak of pragmatic *realpolitik* in the way you present yourself to potential clients. Early in my sparring practice, I was reluctant to accept the Central-Dogma-based starting frame that clients came to me with. I felt the urge to challenge them: *what if you're the problem? What if it's the system and these other people are basically good and competent? What if this isn't zero-sum but win-win?* I learned the hard way that this is not a good idea for two reasons.

First: it's a bad idea to challenge a client's starter frame until there's serious reason for doubt or an obviously better frame is apparent. Unless the assumption that other people are the problem leads to bad contradictions and failures, take that initial diagnosis at face value and run with it.

Second: if people with other problems and requiring other approaches are getting past your first-call filter, you're not actually ready for sparring and you'll fail anyway. Challenging the Central Dogma is a way of second-guessing your own gatekeeping gut feelings.

In general, if the problem is not "other people," chances are you'll be able to tell very quickly in the first exploratory call. In that case you should politely decline with a suggestion like "sounds like you need a therapist/life coach/executive coach/domain expert in X, not a sparring partner." In the first three cases, it is very unlikely that you can serve in those roles (they call for different personality types, as I've talked about before) and should therefore refer the person to someone else.

In the last case, domain expertise, you *may* want to accept, but then it's not primarily a sparring engagement, it's a mislabeled sparring engagement lead that just happens to match your domain expertise.

THE PROBLEM SOCIAL GRAPH

In any sort of engagement, not just sparring, you're talking about, and through, problems. These problems involve the following variables:

1. the client
2. you
3. other people, individually named or local "types"
4. the problem, like "growth is flat" or "the new product is delayed" or "we need to design this new initiative"

What makes it a sparring engagement is that you simplify the first two variables by assuming that neither you nor the client is part of the problem. If that assumption, based on the Central Dogma, turns out to be wrong, then the engagement should end as a sparring engagement, and likely not be handled by you.

This leaves the other two factors. How should you model them? If you're talking to younger people new to leadership roles, or middle management in larger companies, there's a very good chance that the hard part is the problem itself, possibly because they haven't encountered that kind of problem before, and you have, at least secondhand. These are the easiest sparring engagements: help them solve the problem-problem, and the people problems resolve themselves. If you're talking to an experienced senior executive, though, the chances are quite low that the nominal problem is in fact the problem. The problem is nearly always other people. This means you have to model the people situation.

Enter the *Problem Social Graph* or PSG. In this, *you only include people who are relevant to the problem.* And though you might find it a hostile starting default, *you have to assume that everyone on the graph is part of the problem until proven not to be.*

In my case, people sometimes come to me with one of my own frames in mind,[1] but usually they have their own archetypes as well. The Central Dogma of Sparring illustration at the beginning of this chapter illustrates four common problem-social-graph archetypes—but these are by no means exhaustive:

1. *Bozos* (as in Steve Jobs' "flipping the bozobit") are fundamentally compromised by being clueless or otherwise being too disoriented to either work with or fix, and must be worked around.

2. *Sociopaths* (as in *The Gervais Principle*) are ambitious, politically sophisticated, manipulative people looking out for their own interests rather than the organization's, and might not be interested in seeing the problems solved.

3. *Psychopaths* are messed-up people for whom work in the organization is just a convenient place to pursue dark impulses like sadism, sexual exploitation, and so forth (careful: often psychopaths present deceptively, as weaklings or passive-aggressive types).

4. *Monsters* are people explicitly but covertly pursuing agendas that are actively antithetical to the organization's mission, such as fraud, industrial espionage, pure revenge motives aimed at specific people, and so on.

5. *Good ones* are people who show signs of being part of the solution. Often this has strong overlap with people the client likes, gets along with, and is allied with, but the actual definition is: *people who already believe in whatever you and the client agree is the right answer to the problem.*

Yes this is a bleak set of archetypes with which to initially populate the problem social graph, but things are not quite as bleak as they might look. Remember, you're modeling a specific set of *problems*, not a healthy situation. You're not modeling the organization as a whole, or its healthy but irrelevant parts. You're leaving out people irrelevant to the problem—and quite often this leaves out a lot of the good people, because good people usually find ways to do their jobs despite adverse environments. This means the only "good ones" left in the problem graph are ones who are trapped by the problem itself, unable to function effectively.

You're isolating the problem subgraph of a larger social graph and you're starting with the assumption that you actually have a sense of the right answer to the problem.

PROBLEM GRAPH ANALYSIS IS NOT TRIBAL ANALYSIS

That last point is something that is often missed by what I call the tribal school of management analysis. This is a school of thought that tends to ignore the content of the problem and the situational potential for actual right and wrong answers.

The tribal school takes a *both-sides* approach to all tribes vying for control in a situation and, for better or worse, treats the problem as one of reconfiguring tribal boundaries or using tribal conflict patterns to help their client win. Being right or wrong about actual problems is irrelevant in this frame. What matters is being more skilled at tribal warfare to ensure your solution prevails, *regardless of whether it is the right solution or not.* Occasionally, this is the right approach in a sparring engagement, but that's actually surprisingly rare. Usually, one of the tribes is actually *right* about the world, and what needs to be done, in a way that will only become apparent later. So a good filter criterion for accepting clients is whether they think they have a right answer to an interesting problem, or are merely trying to score a tribal victory.

If you are interested in identifying and working with people who are right, and helping them win by virtue of being right, you're in problem-solving mode rather than tribal analysis mode.

This is not idealism, it is laziness. Being actually right about a problem is usually the biggest factor in being able to solve it easily, not power, executive sponsorship, resources, or tribal affiliations. It is odd that this needs to be said explicitly. The only company I know of that does so is Amazon: one of their leadership principles is "Good leaders are right, a lot."

While the setup above might look like it's a fancy way of mapping out the in-group/out-group tribal boundaries relative to your client and modeling a tribal-politics problem, it's not. It's about mapping out the *problem* boundaries on the *social graph.*

If you've picked the right sort of client to work with, their judgment of "good ones" is likely to be good or at least consistent with your own definition of "good ones." It is also likely to rest on an opinion about a set of right answers to problems rather than simple personal likes/dislikes. The ones labeled "good ones" on the graph, as I said, are the ones who believe in the right answer you and the client believe in.

If there's a tribal dynamic at work, you're already part of it ideologically and it's not a part of the problem *per se.* For example, I usually end up in the product-driven tribe within a company rather than the customer-driven tribe, and allied with technical people rather than sales or finance people. This is because I actually believe they are right more often and should have more agency in organizations and run the show. This means my sparring practice is an ongoing test of my own beliefs about businesses and management, and a way of being scientific about any appreciative knowledge I bring. As a sparring partner, I'm not neutral. I spar my management ideology, so to speak.

Second, problem graph roles are often *already* real, simply by virtue of being believed in by your client. The way your client is already dealing with the problem has trusted people they're deploying as part of their current solution (you'll almost never walk into a blank slate situation where something isn't already being tried), and "problem" people they're trying to fence out in one way or the other. This is a given part of the problem definition. Going against the grain of the problem social graph as it already exists is costly—so work with it unless you figure out that it is wrong. In other words, the problem social graph is as much descriptive as normative, because it's already become embodied in the situation by the time you walk in as a sparring partner.

This does not mean tribal analysis is useless. There are times when there is more than one way to be right. There are times when tribal dynamics themselves are the problem and there's no separate objective problem. Solve the tribal problem and the other problems go away. For those situations, there is plenty of literature out there:

- Art Kleiner, *Who Really Matters*
- Dave Logan, *Tribal Leadership*
- Seth Godin, *Tribes*
- Bruce Bruno de Mesquita, Alastair Smith, *The Dictator's Handbook*

Of these, the only one I actually recommend you read (though you should be familiar with all of them) is the last one, which is both brilliant and very useful when tribal analysis *does* apply as the proper framework.

But sparring is rarely about tribal conflict. Pure tribal problems tend to be both simple and boring. There is nothing interesting to be right or wrong about. Outcomes merely tell you who is favored by fortune; they don't teach you something new and true about the world.

Solving pure tribal problems tends to be about making the right friends, the right enemies, buying off some people, cutting off other people, firing, and hiring. Pure social boundary shaping. There's surprisingly little to spar about. Either you have enough authority within the problem scope to reshape the tribal structure or you don't. You have to either fall in with somebody else's tribal agenda or leave the situation. Often, people call me *after* they've already figured out and solved the tribal part of the problem with a reorg or layoffs/hires, and are finally face-to-face with the actual problem.

What if after solving the tribal problem, there's nothing else left to solve? That's a pure tribal problem. I'll make a stronger assertion that I'm less confident about:

If a problem becomes a pure tribal-analysis problem, it's generally not worth solving for intellectual interest, only for material rewards like money. If the problem is a pure tribal problem, you're very likely in some sort of Hobbesian endgame of market harvesting and extraction. There is no real vision or wealth-creation activity underway that makes problems interesting and worth solving.

A good sign is that sales or finance people dominate utterly. If you're working with clients who are part of what I consider the creative, innovative side of the house—mainly engineering and marketing—chances are there are actual problems to be solved, that are worth solving, with right or wrong answers.

SPARRING AS ANTI-THERAPY

Let me close with one more remark on problem social graphs. In transactional analysis, the condition *I'm okay, you're okay* is the foundation of healthy, game-free relationships that are rewarding to all parties within them. This means sparring is a sort of anti-therapy, where you're helping create broader positive effects from a healthy relationship between you and the client—two healthy people.

But there's still a problem. It's just not a therapy problem. And odds are (based on the priors that lead to sparring engagements) it's a people problem created by some good people being right, and some problem people being wrong, about something real.

There may be tribal dynamics involved, but they're not the main focus. The focus is figuring out the right answers, finding the people who believe in them, or can be persuaded to, and acting on them to solve problems, thereby learning whether you were *actually* right.

Helping the truth prevail, in short. Of course this is an idealization. Of course both you and your client have your share of psychological problems. Of course people you cast in various roles informally—bozos, sociopaths, psychopaths, monsters, good ones—are more than those reductive analytical labels you attach to them. Of course you might be wrong about your solutions to the problems. But the starting point is preparing to act, by setting up a problem social graph, based on the belief that you're right rather than wrong. Sounds tautological but it's surprising how many people don't get this.

This is a simple problem setup that will of course change as you think it through. Often, apparent "good ones" will be relabeled part-of-the-problem people. Less often, as you understand a situation, people initially tagged "problem people" might suddenly appear in a new light as part of the solution, or at least not relevant to the problem: red herrings.

These reconfigurations and relabelings are why it is not a tribal analysis problem. The graph changes as your understanding of the problem improves, with new facts becoming apparent. Behaviors presumed to be "bad" turn out to have harmless explanations, while other behaviors presumed to be "good" come to be seen as harmful. Working through this process like a detective solving a murder, gradually getting the right problem social graph converge with the right problem framing and solution, acting on the answers you discover, and learning whether they improve the situation or worsen it—that's the essence of sparring.

This means success at sparring often amounts to setting up the initial problem social graph approximately correctly early and refining it well as you progress. If you tend to get your initial setup very wrong very often, you're not going to be effective as a sparring partner. Badly misreading a situation is not a good look for a sparring partner. In other words, *good sparring partners are right, a lot.* Just like leaders at Amazon are expected to be. This is the test of the knowledge you bring to sparring.

---

1. Most often sociopaths, clueless, losers, which I developed in *The Gervais Principle*, though I have others.

32

BUILDING A SPARRING BUSINESS
WRAPPING UP THE EXECUTIVE SPARRING SERIES

LET'S wrap up this series on sparring. First, a quick summary of the ideas so far. First, in *Introduction to Executive Sparring*, I set up the basic idea and explained how it is different from things like coaching, how and where you can learn the skill, and what traits it takes to be good at it.

Then, in *The Guru Factor*, I explored what kind of epistemic posture is appropriate for sparring (you bring an *appreciative view on instrumental knowledge* as an *emissary of the adjacent possible*) and how to manage perceptions (including self-perceptions) around labels like *Guru* and *Pundit* so you can be effective. And in *The Sparring Arena*, I explored how to set up what I call the *problem social graph* as the context for the sparring, based on the operating assumption that your client is not the problem, other people in their organization are.

In those first three parts, I circled, but never quite got to what I consider to be the solid knowledge foundation on which to build a sparring business. So let's wrap up the series by addressing that topic. The key is the big question I set up in the second part: *what are you a guru of?*

GURU FACTORS VS. BRANDS

This is one of those questions where if you know the answer, you know it immediately and unambiguously. If you have any doubts at all, you haven't figured out the answer. You'll know it's the right answer because you'll feel both trapped by it, and detached from it. It will be something you're neither proud of, nor ashamed of. It's something like blood type rather than height or looks. It's just a fact about you that is overwhelmingly salient to your indie consulting business.

In my case, if you've been following my writing/blogging career, the answer is obvious, I'm viewed as a guru of pragmatic organizational politicking. The perception kicked in with the Gervais Principle series that launched both my writing and consulting careers in 2009, and I've never been able to either get away from it, or significantly recenter around something else. There are a bunch of side dishes I offer alongside the main course:

- "Fat" thinking over lean
- OODA loop stuff
- Software eating the world
- Working with the Silicon Valley management playbook
- Self-aware mediocrity as an executive/managerial ethos

There are also a number of "guru brand attributes," like a strong bias for history, phenomenology, and anecdotal knowledge over abstract theories and process models/frameworks, a cartoonish association with 2x2s (which is something like a signature tell of my style), and so on. But the core has always been pragmatic organizational politicking.

If you are an executive and you know I exist, I'm probably on a fairly short list of people you might call if you're trying to get something ambitious done while dealing with organizational politics along the way. People often want to *talk* to me about lots of other topics, such as TV shows, storytelling, memes, tech trends, and so on, where I can be generally stimulating company. But they only tend to *hire* me when they run into challenges that require modeling and sorting out organizational politics and understanding what peer executives are doing/trying to do, and why. And how to work for, against, with, or around them as necessary, to do what you want to do. The thing about being subject to this sort of perception is that:

1. You *have* to have one to have a sustainable sparring career
2. You *will* hate it for a while once you find it, and feel pigeonholed by it
3. You *must* come to terms with it and kinda ironically own it to enjoy it

You'll know you've found your guru factor when you see people referring to you as "that ___ guy" and you react with a slight cringe, but then shrug. When it's easier for people to remember your shtick than your name, you've found your guru factor. For a lot of people, I am "that guy who wrote that thing about *The Office.*" Even if your name is easier to remember than mine, your shtick will overwhelm it.

Note though, that your guru factor is *not* your personal brand, though the two are closely related. *Your brand is how people remember who you are. Your guru factor is the perspective people come to you for.* By way of analogy, consider something like the Hubble Space Telescope. It has a *brand* as a high-tech, complex, expensive gee-whiz space mission that is a showcase of American technological prowess. Science nerds of all ages love it, and share its photos.

But what people, specifically astronomers, come to it *for* is a specific set of observational capabilities: visible spectrum from LEO, requiring the aperture size Hubble offers. If you wanted a different part of the spectrum, like radio, you'd go sign up for time on a different telescope, even if Hubble is your favorite telescope. If you needed observations that were less sensitive to atmospheric distortions or doable with smaller telescopes, you'd go elsewhere (Hubble doesn't accept observation proposals that can be done by ground-based telescopes). The "unique telescope" analogy also provides a clue as to how to go about developing a guru factor, the thing you're a guru of.

DON'T TRY TO BE "SMART"

This is the most important thing. Nobody ever goes to anybody else for the "smart," perspective to complement their "stupid," one. If you think you're stupid, you look for a therapist or life coach and work on self-esteem issues, not a sparring partner to help you take on the world.

Being smart may or may not be relevant in becoming known for specific perspectives,[1] but people don't come to you for sparring for the smarts. Well, sometimes misguided potential clients do, but the first call goes so awkwardly, they realize it's not actually what they want. This can be very confusing, because many people will *say* they came to because you're "smart," or "sharp," but a little digging will reveal they did not. There's just a lot of general-purpose flattery that goes on in the game of introductions that should not be taken seriously. Even if they genuinely *believe* you're smart, or very smart, that's not why they're there.

Pro tip: the more extreme their adjectives for you, the less they understand their own motives for reaching out to you. Someone who merely says "I wanted to chat with you because you seem like a smart guy" understands their own motives much better than somebody who says, "I wanted to talk to you because you seem like a super-sharp, whip-smart, amazing and unique mind."

Bottomline, "smart" is never part of a guru-factor past a basic minimum. You can't be a moron, but you don't need to be a genius either. Mediocre smarts is the sweet spot.

CONSUME DIFFERENT INPUTS

This is the second most important thing. You learn to see differently—differently enough to sustain a guru-factor shtick—if you're fundamentally consuming different inputs than most people who talk about the things you talk about.

How you see is a function of what you've seen. If you've seen the same things as everybody else, it's hard to see differently from everybody else. But it only has to be different *in the target context.* Watching lots of mainstream TV isn't a particularly rare behavior. That was basically my "seeing training." But it's an unusual perspective in the context of executive business lives. Executives are rarely big TV watchers because it is a time-consuming pastime for lazy people, not one for people putting in 100-hour weeks. So an eye trained by hundreds of hours on the couch consuming sitcoms is different for them.

Of course, you still have to have enough literacy in their domain to make the connections and talk on common ground about the actual problems. I don't spend sparring sessions talking to my clients about my favorite episodes of *The Office.* We talk about whatever they're actually working on or dealing with. For that, I have to do my homework like any other kind of consultant.

"DIFFICULT" IS NOT "DIFFERENT"

This is the third most important thing. If you learn to think well about difficult topics, that makes you an expert. A pundit. People will come to you for definitive, authoritative expertise, not sparring. They'll come to you for advice, and then generally *take it,* because *they* are not competent enough to spar with *you.* Conversely, while you need a basic literacy in difficult topics *they* are experts in, you can't actually spar with them *on* that topic. *You're* not competent. So strangely enough, to uncover a guru factor it's actually better to immerse yourself in topics that are demanding (in terms of being time-consuming) but not actually *difficult*. Mastering difficult subjects puts you on the pundit track, not the guru track. Other doors open, not the sparring door.

For example, I've read a lot of history, and classic older business literature. It's not difficult material, it's just unusual to consume it, since the pop-business literature market is driven by fads and focused on the most recently published books and ideas. So while many people may have *heard* of the "Peter Principle" from 1969, surprisingly few working-age people have actually read the book or even looked it up on Wikipedia. For many people much *older* than me, my 2009 Gervais Principle was actually their first introduction to the idea! So you just have to have put in the time. In my case, since I started consuming this material in the 80s, I know a lot of "old" stuff that most people my age, or even much older, aren't usually familiar with. Most people only get into management literature as adults, and more commonly, when they are actually within striking distance of executive roles. It's not a common teenage-nerd interest, so I accidentally started building an advantageous appreciative knowledge perspective in the 1980s.

THE GURU-PUNDIT DIVIDE

Once you've answered the basic question, *what are you a guru of?* or at least figured out what to watch out for and what behaviors to practice, you can ask whether you actually want to *be* one. If it seems rather late in the game to be asking that question, it's because you don't really understand the question until you have the live option, ready for the exercising, in front of you.

As I've said earlier, I believe having a guru factor going is necessary, but not sufficient, for being a good sparring partner. I've never met a good sparring partner who was *not* a guru of something. To spar, you cannot have a "view from nowhere" of the world. But if you have a live option and you're asking the question at all, chances are, there is an unspoken "do I want to be a pundit instead?" secondary question. You can ask several follow-up questions that clarify this, which I listed in Part 2.

1. Is your relationship to appreciative knowledge closer to punditry or gurudom? Here's a test to tell apart gurus and pundits. In their relationship to appreciative knowledge, *pundits prioritize taste, while gurus prioritize insight.* Recall that I defined pundits as people with an instrumental view of appreciative knowledge, as opposed to gurus who have an appreciative view of instrumental knowledge.

If your relationship to appreciative knowledge is grounded in taste and aesthetics, and you appreciate the beauty in a knowledge domain, you're better suited to being a pundit. You will automatically gravitate towards difficult domains that demand smarts. You will automatically consume the same things others do, but develop a reputation for being a *tastemaker,* who declares which subset of commonly consumed information is good or bad. You will naturally want to cast what you know in the form of polished workshops and glossy printed artifacts.

A guru on the other hand, prioritizes discovery of aha! insights, and doesn't much care who discovers them, gets credit for them, or what the discovery says about their smarts. This is an ideal posture for sparring, since insights usually pop up as part of the process and don't say anything much in particular (whether flattering or unflattering) about who uncovered it. It's like going on a hike with a friend where one of you points out an eagle in a tree. It is something of an accident who gets to spot the eagle. The point is going on a hike where interesting things can be spotted.

2. Is gurudom what you actually want? Though the popular modern image of a guru is a cult leader who mesmerizes a flock of brainwashed morons, the term actually refers to someone people argue with, and this is the connotation that has carried over to *business guru.* Where the guru is a teacher of young novices, the aim is to get good enough to argue with the teacher. This is not actually a pleasant thing for everybody. Many people prefer and expect to be *deferred to.*

A pundit is someone people defer to. If *that's* really what you want, that's what you should cop to, and aim to be. Master a difficult domain that takes smarts. Start a newsletter to bestow wisdom unto the world. Make declarations that follow the rough template: *This thing is good, that thing is bad. Do this, don't do that.* It's a good hustle, and I admire people who do it well. It's just not something I can do.

3. If you somehow ended up on the wrong side of that divide relative to your natural inclinations, how do you cross over? To quote the second part of this series again:

> Punditry is the result of *an instrumental approach to appreciative knowledge.* Gurudom by contrast, is the result of *an appreciative approach to instrumental knowledge.*

For completeness of the 2x2, *an appreciative approach to appreciative knowledge* makes you a *critic*, and *an instrumental approach to instrumental knowledge* makes you a *vocational learner.* Statistically speaking, I'd say about 60% of the population is vocational learners with little to no interest in appreciative knowledge of any sort. Another 30% is critics, focused almost exclusively on consumption tastes, whether or not they are connoisseurs. Of the remaining 10%, I'd say 9% are pundit types, and only 1% are guru types. This has nothing to do with being unique or special. Gurus are rare because few people are lazy and unambitious enough to hang out on the sidelines, appreciating interesting doings without moving to participate consequentially in them.

Most people have an agency itch. They want to energetically *do* stuff. Even the critics are way more energetic than the gurus. They energetically consume and analyze what they consume in excruciating detail. All the wine nerds I know are extremely energetic people. All the pundits I know are voracious and hard-working readers and judges of difficult, demanding material. If you're reading this at all, you're unlikely to be a purely vocational learner or a critic. Chances are, you're either a natural pundit or a natural guru. 9:1 you're a pundit.

If so, you'll probably be miserable sparring. You'll experience the persistent impulse to speak with careful authority rather than in spitballing mode. You'll feel more comfortable when you can occupy a "professional" role in a situation ("Alice here is our machine learning consultant") rather than am amateur hobo role ("Bob here is this guy I met on Twitter who I thought would be interesting to have in this conversation"). When you have to ask a question, you'll feel a slight twinge of reluctance at having to admit to not knowing the answer already. You'll get a little dopamine hit whenever people defer to, or validate your sense of expertise, by accepting your recommendations without question.

This is a pundit trapped in a guru role. I mean, seriously, this is fine. If this is you, go there. Be the pundit. Don't try to occupy sparring roles. Find a box you feel valued and comfortable in, claim it as your own, and live in it. Exercise the influence that will accrue to you if you're good at things you claim to be good at. Get yourself out of sparring conversations and simply reserve the right to distance yourself from decisions you don't agree with, but don't want to get into arguments about.

On the other hand, if being the professional makes you uncomfortable, if being asked to make a decision for others makes you wary, if having your expertise validated makes you instinctively say self-deprecatory things to mitigate the perception of expertise, if you get a genuine kick out of being the hobo in the room . . . you might be a guru trapped in a pundit role.

PUTTING IT ALL TOGETHER

I realize this four-part series hasn't exactly been a cookbook recipe for building a sparring practice. It's been more of a field guide to recognizing it happening to you, and some hints on what to do more or less of to increase or decrease the chances of it happening to you. But to put it all together, the way to build a sparring practice is ... to spar.

Spar at every opportunity, in every available context, with any and all comers. Whether you're being paid or not. Don't stand on ceremony. Don't assume arguing with random people on Twitter is a waste of your time. Don't set uppity conditions and criteria around who is or is not worth arguing with. Standards of competence are for pundits.

Don't let your sense of your own expertise stop you from sparring with anyone unless it's down to not even having a shared vocabulary. And the funny thing is, if you let lack of shared language stop you, you probably don't want to spar anyway. People who want to spar generally find a different language if necessary. If you have a Ph.D. in a jargon-heavy field, but someone random who lacks the jargon says something insightful about it, you'll find a way to engage and spar.

Sparring is like writing. You can't set out to "be a writer." All you can do is write. And more importantly, rewrite. For sparring, the equivalent of rewriting is simply taking notes and reviewing them periodically, maintaining threads of continuity through extended conversations across many sparring sessions.

Log the hours and the notes and *enjoy* it. Do it long enough and people start coming to you to spar about particular things. At some point a guru factor pops and you have to get over hating it and coming to terms with it. Then at some point you find people want to pay you to spar with you. Don't make it too complicated. Keep it caveman simple. Taking a cue from Dan Harmon's story circle,[2] here's my attempt to reduce it to just eight words:

1. *Spar* as much as you can.
2. Take *notes*.
3. *Enjoy* it.
4. Find a *guru* factor.
5. *Choose* to be a guru rather than a pundit.

6. Accept that you'll *hate* it for a while.
7. Come to *terms* with it.
8. *Charge* money for it.

Spar. Notes. Enjoy. Guru. Choose. Hate. Terms. Charge. That's all there is to it. That's how you build a sparring practice. You just have to do it for long enough.

---

1. Obviously, if you are known for surprising neuroscience metaphors, you have to be smart enough to do neuroscience.
2. channel101.fandom.com/wiki/Story_Structure_101:_Super_Basic_Shit

Made in United States
North Haven, CT
13 October 2023

42725773R00178